A Field Guide to the Wildlife of South Georgia

Robert Burton

EDITOR

T0339105

John Croxall

EDITORIAL CONSULTANT

PRINCETON
UNIVERSITY
PRESS

South Georgia
HERITAGE TRUST
PUBLISHING

WILDGuides

All profits from the sale of this book will support conservation work in South Georgia

Published by Princeton University Press,
41 William Street, Princeton, New Jersey 08540
In the United Kingdom: Princeton University Press, 6 Oxford Street,
Woodstock, Oxfordshire OX20 1TW
nathist.press.princeton.edu

Requests for permission to reproduce material from this work should be sent to
Permissions, Princeton University Press

Copyright © 2012 South Georgia Heritage Trust.

Copyright in the photographs remains with the individual photographers.

All rights reserved. No part of this publication may be reproduced, stored in a
retrieval system, or transmitted, in any form or by any means, electronic, mechanical,
photocopying, recording, or otherwise, without the prior permission of the publishers.

British Library Cataloging-in-Publication Data is available

Library of Congress Control Number 2012933830

ISBN 978-0-691-15661-3

Production and design by **WILD**Guides Ltd., Old Basing, Hampshire UK.
Printed in Singapore

10 9 8 7 6 5 4 3 2 1

CONTENTS

SOUTH GEORGIA WILDLIFE

INTRODUCED MAMMALS

INVERTEBRATES

PLANTS 150

Forbs: Non-grasslike herbs

Forbs: Introduced species

Grasses

Sedge

Rushes

The following annotations are used on the species pages.

On the plates

f   female

m   male

j   juvenile

cb   breeding plumage

nb   non-breeding plumage

Conservation status for bird and mammal species has been taken, with permission, from the *IUCN Red List of Threatened Species* (**www.iucnredlist.org/apps/redlist**) © 2011 International Union for Conservation of Nature and Natural Resources.

Population and range

SG   Breeding pairs on South Georgia

GP   Breeding pairs worldwide

GR   global range of invertebrates and plants

Measurements of head and body length and wingspan, where appropriate, are given to provide an indication of animal's size and allow comparisons with other species.

The use of *scientific names* is explained on page 188.

Preface

South Georgia is the most spectacular of the world's subantarctic islands – combining dramatic scenery with vast concentrations of stunning wildlife as well as important but less visible or well-known species. It is also the subantarctic island most visited by tourists. Yet there has never been a comprehensive guide to the wildlife of South Georgia.

The South Georgia Heritage Trust (SGHT), with its objectives of promoting the conservation of the island's natural environment and advancing public education of its heritage, has now filled this gap.

The production of this book was only possible with the help and generosity of many individuals and organisations, and we hope it will enrich the knowledge and experience of visitors to South Georgia.

While the primary aim of the guide is to help visitors identify and learn more about the wildlife they see on their visits, thereby adding to their enjoyment, we also hope it will increase general awareness of the conservation challenges at South Georgia. We hope it will encourage more people to help the SGHT and the Government of South Georgia and the South Sandwich Islands take all necessary steps to protect the island's wildlife in perpetuity and, as far as possible, to help restore it to its former even greater glories. Everyone who buys this guide automatically becomes a supporter of this vision. All proceeds will go directly to support South Georgia conservation through the activities of the South Georgia Heritage Trust.

The guide is 'work in progress' because new species of animals and plants are being added to the South Georgia list, the populations of known species change and new insights are gained into their habits and ecology. We have endeavoured to make the information presented here accurate to the time of publication.

ABOVE: Wandering Albatrosses courting.
LEFT: A colony of King Penguins in winter.

South Georgia and the South Sandwich Islands is an Overseas Territory of the United Kingdom. The territory includes the Shag Rocks and Clerke Rocks and is surrounded by a Maritime Zone whose boundary is 200 nautical miles around these islands. The government of the territory, headed by a Commissioner, is based in Stanley, Falkland Islands, and there are Government Officers based on South Georgia. Two small research stations operated by the British Antarctic Survey, at King Edward Point (*lower left*) and Bird Island are manned permanently.

Topography and Geology

South Georgia is a long, narrow, mountainous and glaciated island (approximately 170 km long by 2 to 40 km wide) situated 1390 km east-south-east of the Falkland Islands.

The island lies on the Scotia Arc, a submarine ridge that links South America with the Antarctic Peninsula, between 35° 47' to 38° 01' West and 53° 58' to 54° 53' South. There are four principal outlying islands, Main Island in the Willis Islands and Bird Island off the north-west tip, Cooper Island off the south-east tip and Annenkov Island to the south-west. There are also numerous islets and rocks.

The island was formed by continental drift when the Atlantic Ocean opened. An extension of the Pacific Plate drove between the South American Plate and the Antarctic Plate to form the Scotia Sea with the Scotia Ridge on the eastern border. The rocks are sedimentary shales and sandstones formed by erosion of volcanoes originating to the west of the island, except for the older granite, basalt and metamorphic rocks in the Drygalski Fjord and Cooper Bay area. These have been heavily folded in some places. Fossils are rare except on Annenkov Island and a few other places.

Half the island is covered in ice and permanent snow, and several glaciers run into the sea. Two mountain ranges, Allardyce and Salvesen, form the backbone of South Georgia. The highest peak is Mt. Paget (2934 m). The coast is largely cliffbound but, on the northern coast especially, there are deep fjords and bays often with areas of flat ground behind them. They make sheltered anchorages for ships and the sites for whaling stations. There are about 20 lakes and many smaller pools. Streams and some short rivers run to the sea.

Glacial scenery showing a lagoon carved out by the ice and dammed by the terminal moraine.

Stacks of lenticular clouds are a familiar feature of South Georgia's weather.
They form downwind of mountain ranges where the wind is thrown into a standing wave.

Climate

South Georgia's position south of the Polar Front (formerly known as the Antarctic Convergence) gives it a more antarctic climate than expected for its latitude. It is affected by a stream of depressions moving eastwards across the Scotia Sea. The climate is essentially cold, cloudy, wet and windy and the weather is very variable. The south-west coast and the mountains intercept the worst of the weather and the north-east side of the island is milder and drier. Snow and rain occur in all seasons but snow does not lie for long in summer. The north-east coast is noted for sudden strong winds which can be especially hazardous for small boats. These may be föhn winds flowing down mountainsides which are accompanied by sudden and very rapid rises in temperature, or winds that are funnelled and accelerated to 100 kph or more by temperature inversions as they cross the mountains.

Long-term records maintained at King Edward Point show an average annual temperature of +1·8°C, ranging from −19·4°C to +26·3°C, and an annual rainfall of 160 cm. The sea sometimes freezes in sheltered bays and pack-ice from the Weddell Sea occasionally reaches South Georgia.

The Fertile Sea

The huge populations of seabirds and seals that breed on South Georgia, and the large numbers of whales that once visited to feed offshore, depend on the fertility of the seas around the island.

The Antarctic Circumpolar Current that sweeps around Antarctica and funnels through the Drake Passage and the current that comes up from the Weddell Sea mix around South Georgia. Their waters are rich in nutrients, especially nitrates, phosphates and silicates, on which myriads of microscopic plants, the phytoplankton, thrive. The sea immediately around South Georgia is particularly fertile because the nutrient-rich currents are brought up from the deep into shallow water where long hours of summer daylight provide the energy for photosynthesis. Productivity is also increased by iron, an essential nutrient, being washed into the sea from the land. Large areas of the Southern Ocean are deficient in iron, which makes them marine deserts. The iron that is available around South Georgia makes it a marine oasis.

The phytoplankton feeds small, floating animals, the zooplankton, especially Antarctic Krill. The zooplankton swarms in the upper levels of the sea and feeds the birds and mammals, as well as fish and squid, which in turn also feed the birds and mammals.

The hordes of penguins and seals breeding ashore are a sign of a fertile sea.

The volcanic landscape of barren rock and steaming fumaroles is the breeding ground for over a million penguins.

South Sandwich Islands

The South Sandwich Islands form a chain of 11 small islands lying on the Scotia Arc approximately 500 kilometres south-east of South Georgia. All have been formed by volcanic action and are composed of basalt and lava. Most have erupted in historic times and Mount Belinda on Montagu Island erupted between 2001 and 2007, releasing a lava flow that ran into the sea and increased the area of the island.

Shag Rocks lie on the shipping route to South Georgia.

Visits to the South Sandwich Islands are infrequent. There are no sheltered anchorages and landings are difficult. Except for the four smallest, the islands are largely ice-covered but even the clear areas are bare rock. Vegetation is scant and consists mainly of mosses, lichens and algae, with occasional small clumps of Antarctic Hair-grass. By contrast, the vegetation around the volcanic fumaroles is very lush and shows a zonation related to the temperature gradient around each fumarole.

The barren nature of the islands is no deterrent to nesting seabirds. Eighteen species have been recorded as breeding, including five species of penguins. Chinstrap Penguins are especially numerous, with a recent estimate of 1·5 million pairs, mostly on Zavodovski Island.

Shag Rocks and Clerke Rocks

Shag Rocks lie 250 km west-north-west of South Georgia and consist of six steep, pointed rocks, the highest reaching 71 m above sea level. Shag Rocks are stained white with the guano of 2000 pairs of nesting Imperial Shags. This is the only nesting species but many other seabirds feed in the vicinity. The rocks lie on the route from the Falkland Islands to South Georgia and are frequently visited by cruise ships.

Clerke Rocks lie 65 km to the south-east of South Georgia. They are very rarely visited and landing is very difficult. Macaroni Penguins, Black-browed Albatrosses and Antarctic Fur Seals are known to breed and a few other species of birds are suspected of breeding.

The Maritime Zone

A 200 nautical mile (370 km) maritime zone around South Georgia and the South Sandwich Islands was proclaimed in 1993. Shag Rocks are included within the zone to the west of South Georgia. Within the zone all fishing must be licensed by the Government of South Georgia and the South Sandwich Islands which enforces international regulations on quotas and fishing techniques, including those for reducing the incidental mortality of seabirds.

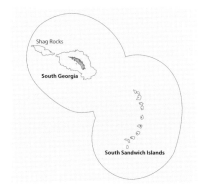

History of Exploitation

South Georgia is renowned for its globally important wildlife. Despite the protection it receives from its remoteness (access is possible only by sea) and absence of permanent human population, its wildlife has, nevertheless, suffered since its discovery. The swarming colonies of penguins, albatrosses and seals that delight visitors belie the fact that some species are in decline. Human activities can be blamed for at least some of the declines. Not only has South Georgia been exploited for its marine resources, introduced animals have, as in so many parts of the world, wrought havoc among native species.

Three trypots and the remains of a stone-walled building show that the sheltered harbour of Elsehul was a centre for sealing.

Trypots were used for rendering oil from seal blubber. The flat face enabled two pots to be placed side-by-side on the furnace.

Sealing

Captain James Cook landed on South Georgia in 1775 and his report on the numbers of fur seals led to the first sealers arriving in 1786. In less than 50 years an estimated 1·2 million fur seal

The recovery of the fur seals following near extinction has brought its own problems. Trampling destroys the tussac habitat where several species of birds nest.

pelts had been taken and the species was commercially, and very nearly biologically, extinct. In addition, sealers also rendered down elephant seal blubber for oil. In 1909 legislation protected fur seals and their breeding grounds, so ending the fur seal industry in South Georgia and allowing their eventual recovery. There are now over 3 million fur seals on the island.

Japanese whalers flense blubber from a Sei Whale in 1964.

Whaling

In 1904 the Norwegian Carl Anton Larsen established the whaling station at Grytviken. His operation was so successful that a further six stations were established by 1913 and South Georgia became the whaling capital of the world. In 1906 a licensing system limited the number of whales caught, protected females with calves and later required that the entire carcass be utilised. The introduction of pelagic factory ships in 1925/26 allowed whalers to operate in the open sea beyond the jurisdiction of the government. Whaling in the Southern Ocean became a free for all, although a few shore stations on South Georgia continued to operate. In addition to hunting whales, the whaling company at Grytviken exploited elephant seals under licence. Closure of the whaling stations was due to whale numbers being too low for the industry to be profitable. Over 175,000 whales had been processed on the shores of South Georgia in 60 years.

Piles of old bones litter the shore as a grim reminder of the whaling industry.

Fishing

Since the mid-1950s, the waters around South Georgia have attracted commercial fisheries. Within 15 years the fishery for Marbled Rockcod had become commercially unviable. Subsequently all fisheries within the Maritime Zone (*page 15*) were regulated according to conservation measures laid down by the Convention on the Conservation of Antarctic Marine Living Resources (CCAMLR). Annual quotas are now set for the three species being caught: Patagonian Toothfish, Mackerel Icefish and Antarctic Krill. The quotas are set at levels that not only protect the stocks but also will not adversely affect the seabirds, seals and whales that feed on them.

This full-grown Patagonian Toothfish will fetch a high price.

Worldwide, the fishing industry is a very serious threat to albatrosses and petrels. The worst problem is longlining, in which birds seize baited hooks as they are shot overboard and are dragged under and drowned. Unless this incidental mortality is prevented some species of seabirds will become extinct. However, these deaths can be prevented by simple measures on the fishing vessels. The fishing around South Georgia is now exceptionally well managed, and incidental mortality is negligible. The South Georgia toothfish and icefish fisheries, and part of the krill fishery, have been certified by the Marine Stewardship Council, which recognises that they are sustainably managed and in accord with best environmental practice.

Saving seabirds

Nevertheless, South Georgia albatross and petrel populations continue to decline, largely because of interaction with fisheries operating outside the Maritime Zone. The areas with most serious problems for South Georgia birds are fisheries off southern Brazil, Uruguay and northern Argentina. The problem is being directly tackled by BirdLife International's Albatross Task Force (funded by the Save the Albatross Campaign, to which many cruise companies visiting South Georgia contribute). Their team of instructors are working with fishers, fishing companies and government agencies to use the most effective techniques to avoid seabird bycatch in these fisheries.

An albatross seizes a baited hook. Simple techniques can prevent this tragedy.

Introduced animals and plants

The sealers and whalers brought a variety of animals to South Georgia, mainly for food. Rabbits were introduced as early as the 1870s, followed much later by sheep, pigs, goats, horses, cattle, chickens, ducks and geese which were kept at whaling stations. Silver foxes were bred at Grytviken for their pelts. Dogs, cats and even monkeys were kept as pets.

None of these species survived as free-living animals and established long-term populations. Cats roamed free and bred around whaling stations but the last one died at King Edward Point in 1980. Of the deliberate introductions, only Reindeer have been successful. Of three introductions, two herds became established in the early 20th century to provide fresh meat for the whaling communities. Accidental introductions of Brown Rats and House Mice have been made since about 1800 by sealers and later by whalers.

The wildlife on South Georgia is so spectacular that it is easy to overlook the devastation that has been wrought by human interference. Introductions of rats and Reindeer have been particularly devastating. The endemic South Georgia Pipit has been exterminated wherever there are rats and the numbers of burrowing petrels greatly reduced. It is difficult to imagine that the island's bird population was once 10 times larger. Reindeer have caused serious overgrazing, greatly reducing the key tussac habitat and eliminating several native plants, while aiding the spread of the introduced Annual Meadow Grass.

About 70 species of flowering plants have been introduced, of which about 37 still survive. They are mostly 'weeds' that arrived in hay for domestic animals. Some are restricted to the vicinity of the whaling stations but others, such as Annual Meadow Grass, Mouse-ear Chickweed and Dandelion, have spread widely. Introduced plants compete for space with native species

There are even problems with introduced insects. Alien beetles prey on native insects (*page 143*) and recently-arrived hoverflies could assist the spread of some alien plants by pollinating them (*page 146*).

A clump of Cow Parsley at Grytviken.

Habitat Restoration

The South Georgia Heritage Trust and the Government of South Georgia are undertaking very ambitious and far-reaching projects to restore the island's habitat by eradicating the most damaging alien species.

In March 2011 the SGHT made a successful start to the eradication of rats by spreading rat poison over the Greene, Thatcher and Mercer Peninsulas (the areas in Cumberland Bay around Grytviken), together with Saddle Island which had recently become rat-infested. This is already the largest operation of its kind undertaken in the world and it is a race against the glaciers' retreat allowing rats into new areas. If this operation proves successful, as it already appears to be, the rest of the island will be tackled, starting in 2013. The project will not be a success unless every single rat is killed; if any survive they will recolonise the island.

Eradicating rats from South Georgia is possible because glaciers divide the island into isolated areas which can be tackled one at a time.

The project has been designed to reduce the danger to other wildlife to a minimum. Spreading the bait by helicopter is undertaken in late summer after the breeding season and care is taken not to disturb King Penguin colonies. Penguins and most other seabirds do not feed on land so there is no danger of them eating the poison bait. A monitoring programme will check that the rats have gone and the losses of other species are within acceptable limits. Losses are acceptable because of the enormous benefits of getting rid of the rodents.

A helicopter with bait-spreader flies out from Grytviken.

The Government of South Georgia, in an initiative strongly supported by the SGHT, is preparing to eradicate the Reindeer because they must be removed before their range is baited with rat poison. Otherwise they will eat the poison intended for the rats. At the time of writing no decision had been made on how the Reindeer will be removed.

The Government is also attempting to eliminate some alien plant species which have limited distributions, notably the Bittercress and Procumbent Pearlwort around Grytviken.

Retreating glaciers

The retreat of South Georgia's glaciers as the climate changes is potentially a serious problem for wildlife. At the moment the island is effectively divided into several smaller ' islands' formed by the glaciers acting as natural barriers to the spread of animals, plants and disease, both alien and native. This has limited the ranges of rats and Reindeer largely to the western end of the island and the north-east coast, especially to dense coastal tussac habitat and around the whaling stations.

This situation is set to change as the glaciers' effectiveness as barriers declines and most importantly the safe haven of the south coast, currently lacking alien predators, is under threat. Ninety seven per cent of South Georgia's glaciers that terminate in the sea and form effective barriers have retreated in the past 50 years. The majority have retreated up to 500 m, but the Neumayer Glacier has retreated 4·4 km. So areas previously safe from introduced animals are becoming open to colonisation.

The Schrader Glacier in 2011. Only four years earlier it reached the sea so that it was impossible to cross in front of it.

Biosecurity

Invasive or alien species are the greatest single threat to the wildlife of islands. As well as preying on or competing with the native fauna and flora, invasive species may make an island more vulnerable to new invasions. (For example on South Georgia grazing by Reindeer encourages the spread of the introduced Annual Meadow Grass.) South Georgia has been identified as the subantarctic island most vulnerable to alien invasion. This is due to the combination of climate change, the number of visitors and the impact of existing alien species.

It is vital to prevent more alien species arriving at South Georgia and becoming established. Effective biosecurity, defined as measures designed to prevent the introduction of alien species, is required by South Georgia law. So far, the cold environment has limited the establishment of aliens but the warming climate increases the risk of aliens, already present but with a limited 'harmless' range, starting to spread across the island.

To prevent new aliens arriving, biosecurity plans have been made for all types of vessel visiting the island. These include procedures for all visitors and for the resupply of the stations at King Edward Point and Bird Island. Private expeditions must produce their own biosecurity plans to demonstrate their awareness of the risks and suggested methods for mitigation.

The biosecurity facility at King Edward Point is used for checking cargo and equipment arriving on the island. However, there is an emphasis on eliminating aliens from a vessel heading for South Georgia at the point of departure, so they do not even arrive at the island. Ships must be rat-free so there is no risk of them getting ashore if they are wrecked on South Georgia.

Passengers on a cruise ship clean their boots before arriving at South Georgia. They remove mud that might contain seeds or other alien life. It is important that all visitors carry out biosecurity procedures and make a real contribution to the preservation of the island.

Protected Areas and Regulations

It is an offence to kill or harm any animal or damage any habitat or heritage site. Disturbance to wildlife is minimised through permits being required for visits and enforcement of strict codes of conduct. Numbers of visitors to sensitive areas are strictly managed and, if any problem arises, the government can close an area to all visitors with immediate effect.

Specially Protected Areas

1. Willis Islands
2. Bird Island
3. Cape Paryadin Peninsula
4. All rat-free areas including
   a. Albatross Island
   b. Prion Island
   c. Cape Rosa
5. Cooper Island
6. Larsen Harbour
7. Annenkov Island
8. Fanning Ridge Coast
9. Nuñez Peninsula

Sensitive areas of South Georgia are designated as Specially Protected Areas (SPAs). A site can be designated an SPA if its flora or fauna are of significant conservation or ecological importance, it is of significant geological, geomorphological or landscape importance, it is of high scientific research interest; or if it is free of rats. It is an offence to visit an SPA without a government permit. Individual SPAs are managed through Management Plans, which allow specific prohibitions and management actions. Permits to visit some SPAs will only be issued under exceptional circumstances.

Areas of sea are protected by designation as Marine Protected Area (MPAs). These aim to conserve marine flora or fauna, any species dependent on the marine environment, marine habitats or types of marine habitat, features of geological or geomorphological interest or features of heritage interest. Restrictions and prohibitions for an MPA can be set out in a series of Conservation Orders.

The severe effect of grazing by Reindeer is demonstrated by fencing off a plot where plants can regenerate.

Vegetation and Plant Communities

The vegetation of South Georgia may be categorised into 11 principal plant community types (most of which can be subdivided into more specific communities). These are associations of groups of plants which tend to occur wherever the same environmental conditions prevail. The major habitat determinants are: type of substrate (such as rock, gravel, soil or peat), wetness, steepness of slope, aspect, degree of shelter from wind, length of winter snow-lie and nutrient status.

Replacement grassland

This is not a natural community but one that has replaced native communities, formerly dominated by Tussock Grass and Greater Burnet, where they have been excessively grazed by Reindeer. Alien Annual Meadow Grass has rapidly colonised the over-grazed communities and developed locally extensive lawns. The grass benefits from continual cropping by Reindeer and nutrients from their dung. Trampling by Reindeer, fur seals and penguins detaches fragments which spread and take root, aiding its rapid spread. Its spread has also been aided by fur seals. In recent decades the grass has been a primary colonist on the outwash plains below receding glaciers (e.g. at Salisbury Plain and Fortuna Bay), replacing the natural development of fellfield.

Tussac grassland

Tussock Grass is the most widespread community on the island and forms a dark green zone in all coastal areas. Each plant develops a pedestal of peat, often more than 1 m high, from which the foliage rises another metre. In wet areas these tussocks form an almost impenetrable canopy (closed tussac), often eroded at their muddy bases by fur seals. On drier coastal slopes the tussocks become sparser (open tussac) and, away from the nutrient input of the fauna, are a more yellow-green colour. Tussac grassland is the favoured habitat for many species of seabirds, notably albatrosses, burrowing petrels and Gentoo and Macaroni Penguins.

Dry grassland

Short tussock-forming grassland, dominated by Brown or Tufted Fescue, occurs especially on dry hillsides, usually above the coastal tussac zone and most extensive on the sheltered mid-north side of the island. It is a species-rich community with many flowering plants, mosses and macrolichens. It grades into various other communities as the habitat conditions change.

Wet grassland

Raised beaches, glacial outwash plains and other coastal flat areas are dominated by extensive swards of Antarctic Hair-grass and several wet-habitat mosses. The grass is tolerant of trampling by seals and penguins and benefits from the added nutrients.

Bog

Wet valley floors, rock basins and coastal flats beyond the tussac zone are dominated by Brown Rush and several bryophytes (mosses and liverworts). This vegetation decays and forms an acidic peat which, in places, reaches a depth of 2–4 m and has a radiocarbon age of up to 9,500 years old.

Mire

A community dominated by the rusty brown moss *Syntrichia robusta*, Greater Rush and scattered Brown Rush and Greater Burnet on wet seepage slopes. This vegetation does not accumulate deep peat and the underlying soil is only mildly acidic.

Herbfield

This community occurs on sheltered moist slopes and well-drained level areas, and is dominated by Greater Burnet, which often provides a closed canopy of foliage. In less dense stands there is usually an understorey of the moss *Syntrichia robusta*. As the adjacent ground becomes wetter or drier the community grades into other communities.

Fellfield

A pioneer community which favours dry, stony and gravelly habitats on glacial outwash plains, moraines and wind-exposed ridges and slopes. Usually very sparsely vegetated, the dominant species are Brown Fescue, Alpine Cat's-tail, Antarctic Hair-grass and Greater and Lesser Burnet, as well as mosses and lichens.

Bryophyte flushes, stream and pond margins

Many bryophytes (mosses and liverworts) are associated with springs, the margins of streams and the edges of pools and occasionally lakes. They form a narrow but distinctive community of mosses, mats of the liverwort *Marchantia berteroana*, and often a fringe of Greater Burnet, rushes and some other higher plants. At pool margins a floating mat of moss may extend 1–2 metres from the shoreline.

Moss turf banks

Two species of moss (*Polytrichum strictum* and *Chorisodontium aciphyllum*), separately or in association, build up a thick turf with the living moss overlying a loose peat formed by their decaying stems. In drier habitats on gentle slopes *Polytrichum* forms a hard compact surface, often with scattered Greater Rush and Brown Fescue. On wetter slopes, often among open tussac grassland, *Chorisodontium* forms large loose turf mounds.

Lichen and moss rock communities

Boulder fields, screes (talus), cliffs and other rock surfaces usually support a large diversity of lichens. There may be several species of moss, especially where there is water trickling over the rock and beside waterfalls. Coastal cliffs, notably downwind of penguin and other seabird colonies, often have a colourful display of salt spray-tolerant orange crustose lichens which rely on a high nitrogen input from the aerosol of ammonia emanating from the colonies. Many of the species in these communities are often arranged in a series of zones ranging from high tide mark to 50 or more metres above sea level. Inland, and beyond the influence of spray and birds, other associations of lichens and some drought-tolerant mosses create more drab mosaics on the rock surfaces. On wet rocks and ledges a variety of mosses and liverworts predominate.

South Georgia Wildlife

BIRDS

The birds of South Georgia belong to 12 families in six major groups or orders. Nearly all the island's species belong to either Sphenisciformes, the flightless penguins, or Procellariiformes, the tubenosed birds to which the aerial albatrosses and petrels belong.

All breeding species on South Georgia are seabirds except two ducks (the South Georgia Pintail and Speckled Teal), the Snowy Sheathbill and the South Georgia Pipit. The last is unique as the only member on the island of the huge group of passerine or perching birds, and is also the island's only songbird.

TOP LEFT: White-chinned Petrels

TOP CENTRE: South Georgia Pintail

TOP RIGHT: Brown Skuas

MAIN PICTURE: Macaroni Penguins on Bird Island

① King Penguin *Aptenodytes patagonicus*

DISTRIBUTION: South Georgia, South Sandwich Islands (small numbers from recent colonisation), Prince Edward, Crozet, Kerguelen, Heard and Macquarie Islands; also Falkland Islands (small numbers). Vagrant south to Antarctica and north to Australia, New Zealand, Saint Helena, South Africa, Brazil, Uruguay.

Resident	
SG:	> 450,000 pairs
GP:	1–1·5 million pairs
Length:	85–95 cm
Threats: None.	

IDENTIFICATION: The second largest penguin and the largest to breed on South Georgia. The sexes are similar but the female is slightly smaller. The slate-grey back and white front are separated by a narrow black line that extends up to the chin and to the head which are both also black. Two vivid orange auricular patches extend to the throat where they almost, but not quite, meet with a marginally less brilliant gorget of vivid orange. The crown in a freshly moulted bird may be covered with a haze of yellow, which in some lights appears almost green. The bill is long and slim and curves downwards towards the tip. Its sides are covered with brilliant fluorescent yellow plates that are shed during the moult. Immatures resemble adults but have duller auricular and gorget patches of lemon yellow to white. The chicks hatch with dark chocolate-brown down which is replaced in 7–10 days by long brown down. Colour variants are recorded infrequently at South Georgia.

BEHAVIOUR: King Penguins nest in dense colonies. There is no nest and the single egg is incubated on the feet under a flap of skin. Incubating birds stand at pecking distance from each other, although altercations are common when they get too close. This can result in wing flapping or wing beating of neighbours. The breeding cycle is preceded by the moult. Courtship to fledging takes approximately 14 months. Incubation is 55–56 days and fledging about 50 weeks. After 5 weeks chicks gather in crèches. Successful birds may raise two chicks every three years. This unique breeding cycle means that, at some times of year, moulting adults, eggs, young chicks and older chicks near to fledging are present in the colony. Diet is mainly squid and lanternfish caught in dives usually lasting 10 minutes and down around 25 m but occasionally to over 300 m.

VOICE: King Penguins have a broad vocabulary, making a variety of calls both to their partners and to their single chick. The most conspicuous call used for recognition is an ecstatic musical trumpeting, usually voiced with both neck and head extended to the sky and flippers held aloft. Chicks make a whistling call to attract the attention of their parents. Parents and chicks recognise each others' voices.

WHERE TO SEE: The largest colonies are at St Andrews Bay (150,000 pairs), Salisbury Plain (60,000 pairs), Royal Bay (30,000 pairs), Gold Harbour (25,000 pairs) and Fortuna Bay (7,000 pairs). The population is increasing and new colonies have formed in recent years. These are spectacular sights, comparable with any wildlife experience on the planet.

The unique breeding cycle of the King Penguin

King Penguins take more than a year to fledge a chick. Consequently, they cannot raise a chick every year.

The chart shows how a single pair raises no more than two chicks in the three years. They lay an egg at the beginning of summer in Year 1, and fledges the chick the following summer. Food is scarce during the winter, so the adults temporarily abandon the chick to concentrate on feeding themselves. If the chick is old enough and large enough, it survives on its reserves until the parents can resume feeding it.

After the chick has fledged, the pair starts to breed again in Year 2, but this egg is laid much later in the summer. The chick usually does not have time to grow enough to survive the winter food shortage, and eventually dies of starvation. The parents are then free to start breeding early in Year 3, which is a repeat of Year 1.

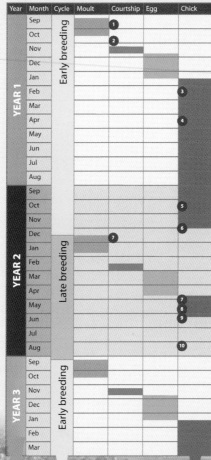

Year	Month	Cycle	Moult	Courtship	Egg	Chick
YEAR 1	Sep	Early breeding		①		
	Oct					
	Nov			②		
	Dec					
	Jan					
	Feb					③
	Mar					
	Apr					④
	May					
	Jun					
	Jul					
	Aug					
YEAR 2	Sep	Late breeding				
	Oct					⑤
	Nov					
	Dec					⑥
	Jan		⑦			
	Feb					
	Mar					
	Apr					
	May					⑦
	Jun					⑧ ⑨
	Jul					
	Aug					⑩
YEAR 3	Sep	Early breeding				
	Oct					
	Nov					
	Dec					
	Jan					
	Feb					
	Mar					

① Adults moult early in spring.

② After moulting, they return to the sea to feed before coming ashore again to court.

③ When the chick is 5 weeks old, it joins other chicks in a crèche.

④ **Food becomes scarce.** The parents abandon the chick from a few weeks to several months.

⑤ **Food becomes plentiful again.** The chick receives food again.

⑥ Chick successfully raised.

⑦ The adults recover from breeding and start again, but later than the previous year.

⑧ Food has become scarce and feeding stops. This time, the young chick has not had time to put on reserves and starves.

⑨ Chick dies at some point during the winter.

⑩ Without a chick to feed, the parents recover their condition and start breeding in early spring.

ABOVE LEFT: A King Penguin inspects the egg balanced on its feet. ABOVE RIGHT: A moulting King Penguin.
BELOW: A crèche of King Penguin chicks in winter.

1 Gentoo Penguin *Pygoscelis papua*

NEAR THREATENED	
Resident	
SG:	Approximately 105,000 pairs
GP:	380,000–390,000 pairs
Length:	75–90 cm

DISTRIBUTION: Antarctic Peninsula and associated island groups, north to South Georgia and subantarctic islands east to Macquarie Island; also Argentina (a few pairs on islands in Beagle Channel). Falkland Islands. Little dispersal in non-breeding season but vagrants have occurred in southern Australia, New Zealand and to 43°S in Argentina. Nests South Sandwich Islands.

IDENTIFICATION: The sexes are similar; male slightly larger. Upperparts and tail are bluish-black; the underparts are white. A white fringe extends between the rump and the tail. The head and throat are black with clearly discernible but variable white patches above each eye that extend over the crown. Each eye-patch also normally meets a distinct white eye ring. There are often scattered white feathers on the head and nape. The feet are pale white-pink. The bill is black with conspicuous orange-red on the sides. The eye is brown.

Threats: In some years, when krill, a main food, is scarce, breeding pairs may raise only a single chick, or in extreme years, none. These krill-scarce years occur once or twice a decade and sometimes entire colonies may fail to produce any offspring. The adults generally recover quickly and usually breed the following season.

WHERE TO SEE: Around the coast.

VOICE: Males often engage in an ecstatic display to attract a mate; the bird stretches its head, neck and body upwards, pointing the bill vertically while trumpeting loudly. The flippers are generally held outstretched and still. Both members of a pair engage in a mutual display which is similar to the ecstatic display. Birds will also gently hiss at each other, particularly at nest relief.

BEHAVIOUR: Nests are bulky piles of vegetation and two eggs are laid. The onset of egg-laying can be highly variable between years. If a pair loses its clutch, they may relay. Eggs are laid from early October to early November. Incubation is 38 days and fledging 85–117 days (compared with 62–82 days in the Antarctic). Parents attempt to raise both chicks, and are often successful.

Gentoos remain near the colonies all year and feed usually within 10 km of the shore. The diet is fish and crustaceans caught in dives up to 100 m.

NOTE: The world Gentoo Penguin population is undergoing shifts in distribution and there may be a general decline. There may also be considerable fluctuations in one place from year to year linked with the availability of krill.

Chinstrap Penguin *Pygoscelis antarcticus*

DISTRIBUTION: Antarctic Peninsula and associated islands north to South Georgia and Bouvetøya; also on Peter I Øya and Balleny Islands. Chinstrap Penguins are birds of the oceanic subantarctic. Populations are changing southwards along the Antarctic Peninsula, probably as a result of reduced seasonal sea-ice in those areas. Numbers may be decreasing at South Georgia. Modest northwards dispersal after breeding, with vagrants reported from most subantarctic islands and all mainland continental landmasses. Nests South Sandwich Islands

IDENTIFICATION: The sexes are similar. Upperparts and tail are bluish-black, the underparts are white. The forehead is black, although the rest of the face and throat are white or greyish-white. The narrow black line running under the chin from ear to ear gives the bird its common name. The feet are pale pink with black soles. The bill is black. The eye is red-brown.

NEAR THREATENED	
Breeding visitor	
SG:	13,400 pairs and probably decreasing
GP:	7·5 million pairs
Length:	70–75 cm

Threats: Colonies on South Georgia were closed to visitors from 2004 to 2009 because of a suspected outbreak of avian cholera.

WHERE TO SEE: Only a few colonies at South Georgia, mostly at the colder, south-east end of the island in and around Cooper Bay, Cape Disappointment and Pickersgill and Annenkov Islands.

VOICE: Birds often engage in an ecstatic display to attract a mate. The bird stretches its head, neck and body upwards, pointing the bill vertically while making a series of staccato shrill calls that are generally repeated several times. The flippers are generally held outstretched and still. Both members of a pair engage in a mutual display similar to the ecstatic display but consisting more of a series or cackles. Birds also hiss at each other.

BEHAVIOUR: Nests are made of pebbles and there are usually two eggs. They are laid late November to early December and incubated for 31–39 days. Chicks fledge at 48–59 days. Parents attempt to raise both chicks, often successfully.

Porpoising Chinstrap Penguin

① Macaroni Penguin *Eudyptes chrysolophus*

VULNERABLE	
Breeding visitor	
SG:	1 million pairs
GP:	Approximately 6·3 million pairs
Length:	70 cm

Threats: Colonies on South Georgia have declined over the past few decades, possibly as a result of competition for food with Antarctic Fur Seals and changes in ocean dynamics.

WHERE TO SEE: All around the coast, with the largest colonies on the north coast, including Elsehul, and especially on Willis Islands and Bird Island.

DISTRIBUTION: South Georgia is the centre of the population but also common at Prince Edward, Marion, Crozet and Heard Islands. Scattered pairs (usually among Chinstrap Penguins) and small colonies from South Shetland Islands (local) to South Sandwich Islands and Bouvetøya; also Falkland Islands (a few pairs among Rockhopper Penguins) and southern Chile. After breeding and moult population moves north. Nests South Sandwich Islands.

IDENTIFICATION: The sexes are similar; the male is slightly larger. Upperparts and tail are black with a bluish tinge, while the underparts are white. The head and throat are black but with brilliant golden-yellow plumes above each eye originating from a central patch on the forehead and drooping over the eyes. The feet are flesh pink, with blackish soles. The bill is heavy, often ridged, and dark orange-brown. There is a conspicuous bare patch of pink skin that extends from the bill almost to the eye. The eye is garnet-red. The juvenile has grey chin and throat, and the plumes are missing or sparse.

VOICE: In the 'ecstatic' display to attract a mate, the bird stretches upwards, pointing the bill vertically while making a series of braying, raucous cries or trumpeting calls, often also rolling its head from side to side. The flippers are generally held outstretched. The pair engages in a mutual display similar to the ecstatic display.

BEHAVIOUR: Colonies are on steep slopes dropping into the sea. The nests are made of stones and pebbles. Eggs are laid in October and November. Incubation is about 36 days and fledging about 60 days. Macaroni Penguins lay two eggs (*inset*) but it is rare for more than one chick to be raised. The species is unique in that the first 'A' egg is smaller than the second 'B' egg. (In other penguins that lay two eggs, the first is the larger) The 'A' egg is always discarded either on the day that the 'B' egg is laid or the day before. None of the suggested explanations for this phenomenon is completely satisfactory.

Food is krill and other crustaceans, small fish and cephalopods. Foraging trips during incubation average 375 km for females and 575 km for males but are often only about 60 km when rearing chicks.

Porpoising Macaroni Penguins

'A' egg

'B' egg

ABOVE: A pair of Macaroni Penguins preen each other.
BELOW: Gentoo Penguins with half-grown chicks.

ABOVE: Gentoo Penguins coming ashore to roost.
BELOW: A Chinstrap Penguin carries a pebble to its nest.

Emperor Penguin *Aptenodytes forsteri*

Vagrant	
Length:	100–130 cm

DISTRIBUTION: Antarctica, north to islands near base of Antarctic Peninsula.

IDENTIFICATION: The largest living penguin. The sexes are similar; female slightly smaller. Emperor Penguins have a dark grey-blue back and a white front separated by a broad black stripe that extends up towards the chin. The head, chin and throat are black. Bright yellow auricular patches extend down to the throat where they meet with a slightly less bright gorget of yellow. The bill is curved downwards towards the tip; its sides covered with brilliant fluorescent pink, lilac or orange plates that are shed during the moult. The legs and feet are black; the outside of the tarsus is feathered. The eye is brown. Immature has paler upperparts, is white rather than yellow around the head and neck and has a distinctive white chin and throat.

Southern Rockhopper Penguin
Eudyptes chrysocome*

VULNERABLE	
Vagrant and very rare breeder	
SG:	Individuals are occasionally recorded at Macaroni Penguin colonies
Length:	45–58 cm
Threats: Declining in most areas for unknown reasons.	

DISTRIBUTION: Falkland Islands, offshore islands in southern Chile and Argentina, and subantarctic islands.

IDENTIFICATION: The sexes are similar; male is larger. Upperparts and tail are dark slate grey with a bluish tinge, while the underparts are white. The head and throat are blackish but with a bright yellow stripe above each eye extending backwards to form drooping yellow plumes. The feet are pink with black soles. The bill is heavy and dark orange-red. There is a strip of bare skin at the gape. The eye is bright red. Juvenile and immature crest is poorly developed, chin and throat are grey. South Georgia visitors are likely to come from major colonies in the Falkland Islands after breeding and moult finish in February/March, when these populations migrate north and west into the Patagonian Sea.

Royal Penguin *Eudyptes schlegeli**

VULNERABLE	
Vagrant	
SG:	Occasionally recorded at Macaroni Penguin colonies
Length:	65–75 cm

DISTRIBUTION: Restricted to Macquarie Island and nearby Bishop and Clerk Islands.

IDENTIFICATION: Very similar to Macaroni Penguin (*opposite, with Royal Penguin, and page 42*) except for the white face, chin and throat.

*See taxonomic notes page 188.

Adult Emperor Penguins (*left*) are larger than King Penguins (*page 34*), although juveniles (*right*) may be smaller.

The King Penguin has a longer bill and its auricular patches are narrower where they meet the gorget.

Visitors to South Georgia are mostly immatures or post-breeding adults from colonies on the Antarctic Peninsula.

1

1j

The plumes of the larger Macaroni Penguin (*right and page 42*) do not droop and it has pink bare skin at the gape.

2

Macaroni Penguin

3

Adélie Penguin *Pygoscelis adeliae*

Visitor, occasional breeder	
SG:	very few pairs, rarely sighted
GP:	2–2·5 million pairs
Length:	70 cm

DISTRIBUTION: Antarctica, Antarctic Peninsula, north to South Sandwich Islands and Bouvetøya. Little evidence of much dispersal of adults out of sea-ice zone in winter. Juveniles move north but very rarely north of 60°S. Nests South Sandwich Islands.

IDENTIFICATION: The sexes are similar; male slightly larger. Upperparts, head, throat and tail are blue-black. Underparts are pure white. The eye is brown with a conspicuous and distinctive white eye-ring. The bill, mainly black with some orange-red, appears short as the base is covered by feathers. The legs and feet vary from dull white to pink with black soles. The immature has a white chin and throat and a dark eye-ring. It can be confused with an immature Chinstrap Penguin (*page 40*) but the latter has a longer bill with no feathers at the base.

2 Magellanic Penguin

Spheniscus magellanicus

NEAR THREATENED	
Vagrant	
Length:	70 cm

DISTRIBUTION: Breeds on the Atlantic and Pacific coasts of South America and the Falkland Islands. Most populations move northwards along coastal current systems after breeding; vagrants occur widely further north still.

IDENTIFICATION: The sexes are similar; male slightly larger. The head, face, upperparts and tail are brownish black, while the underparts are white. A broad dark band across the chest extends down the flanks to the thighs, and a broad white band on each side of the crown loops behind each eye and joins under the throat. The breast has a variable number of black spots that are individually distinct, while occasional white patches also occur on the back. Birds have bare skin, usually pink, above the bill and around the eyes during the breeding season. The feet are black with pink splodges and have blackish soles. The bill is black with a pale grey band near the tip. The eye is brown with a small red ring, especially in older birds. Immature lacks the characteristic pattern on head and breast.

An immature Adélie Penguin has a white chin and throat, and a dark eye-ring which turns white when approximately one year old.

Tubenoses

The order Procellariiformes or tubenoses is a major group of seabirds found in all oceans of the world. Typically long-winged and excellent fliers, they are adapted for travelling long distances over the sea and usually come ashore only to breed. They get their common name from the long tubular nostrils, which are paired on each side of the bill in albatrosses. Unusually for birds, they have a good sense of smell which is used for finding food.

Half the 100 or so species live in the southern hemisphere and they are the most abundant birds of the Southern Ocean.

The order includes four families: **Diomedeidae** – albatrosses; **Procellariidae** – fulmars; shearwaters and many petrels; **Hydrobatidae** – storm-petrels; and **Pelecanoididae** – diving-petrels.

The Procellariidae includes the prions *Pachyptila* species and gadfly petrels *Pterodroma* species, two groups of small petrels which are very difficult to identify at sea.

ABOVE: An Antarctic Prion showing the tubular nostrils.

RIGHT: A Light-mantled Albatross displays from a cliff ledge.

BELOW: A Southern Giant Petrel feeds on the carcass of a whale.

MAIN PICTURE: A flock of Antarctic Prions.

There are three main groups of albatrosses in the Southern Ocean. The largest albatrosses, with wingspans of up to 3 m or more, of the genus *Diomedea* are known as great albatrosses; they include the **Wandering**, **Royal** and **Tristan Albatrosses**. Smaller albatrosses, often known as **mollymawks**, of the genus *Thalassarche* (formerly placed in *Diomedea*), are distinguished by their much smaller size and the dark 'saddle' linking the dark upper surface of the wings. The dark-bodied, slender-winged **Sooty** and **Light-mantled Albatrosses** of the genus *Phoebetria* are distinctive.

❶ Southern Royal Albatross

Diomedea epomophora

VULNERABLE	
Summer visitor, very rarely seen close to South Georgia	
Length:	110–120 cm
Wingspan:	290–350 cm

DISTRIBUTION: Main breeding population at Campbell Island with small numbers at Auckland Islands. In non-breeding season widely distributed (35–60° S) in the Southern Ocean.

IDENTIFICATION: Similar in plumage to Wandering Albatross. (*page 54*) Head, body and tail of immatures largely white. Upper surface of wing initially blackish, but whitens over time from leading edge. Dark cutting-edge of upper mandible readily visible at close quarters. Follows ships.

❷ Northern Royal Albatross

Diomedea sanfordi

ENDANGERED	
Possible vagrant	
Length:	110–120 cm
Wingspan:	290–350 cm

DISTRIBUTION: Chatham Island and a few pairs on South Island, New Zealand. Interbreeds with Southern Royal Albatross on Enderby Island.

IDENTIFICATION: Similar in plumage to Wandering Albatross (*page 54*) but with solid black upperwings and all-white tail. Juveniles largely like adults but with variable brown on crown, rump and lower back. Dark cutting-edge of bill readily visible at close quarters. Diagnostic black mark on leading edge of underwing near carpal joint.

❸ Antipodean Albatross

Diomedea antipodensis

VULNERABLE	
Vagrant	
Length:	110–120 cm
Wingspan:	280–300 cm

DISTRIBUTION: Breeds on Antipodes, Auckland and Campbell Islands and not usually seen east of the coast of Chile.

IDENTIFICATION: Most adults are dark brown with a white face like a juvenile Wandering Albatross (*page 54*) but old males are paler with black tail and crown. Upper wing entirely dark except, occasionally, a few white feathers. Very difficult to distinguish but perhaps best separated from Wandering Albatross by considerably smaller size and shorter bill.

One individual, ringed as a chick on Antipodes Island, was found on Bird Island in 2010.

Southern Royal Albatross adults most easily distinguished from Wandering Albatross by a white leading edge to wing, all white tail and, at close quarters, the obvious black cutting edge on the upper mandible.

Northern Royal Albatross is distinguished from Southern Royal Albatross by a slimmer body and wings that are more uniformly black without white flecking.

Northern Royal Albatross has a diagnostic black mark on the leading edge of the underwing near the carpal joint.

Antipodean Albatross is smaller than Wandering Albatross.

1 Wandering Albatross

Diomedea exulans *

DISTRIBUTION: Circumpolar breeding distribution, with large populations at four island groups (South Georgia, Crozet, Kerguelen and Prince Edward Islands) and very small numbers at Macquarie Island. Extremely wide-ranging during the non-breeding period (probably more so than other albatrosses), with South Georgia birds throughout Southern Ocean, north to 25°S.

IDENTIFICATION: The largest seabird seen in the region and the only great (*Diomedea*) albatross breeding at South Georgia. When seen together ashore, the female is smaller with a less heavy bill. Shows complex plumage variation. Juveniles have white face from forehead to upper foreneck, but are otherwise dark chocolate brown. Plumage becomes increasingly white with age; however, females tend to remain darker and retain brown cap for longer. Adults largely white on body, with dark vermiculation that reduces with age, especially in males. Upperwings dark, gradually becoming whiter with age from centre. Tail black in immatures, becoming increasingly white with age (although many adults retain a few dark tail feathers or tips). Many Wandering Albatrosses, uniquely, have crescents of pink-stained feathers behind the eyes. Huge pink bill with bulbous tip. Follows ships.

VOICE: Large range of guttural, croaking, whining, gurgling and bill snapping calls made on land, particularly during displays. Guttural, croaking and bill snapping calls also used at sea.

BEHAVIOUR: Extremely long-lived (some to > 50 years) and with a mean age of first breeding of 10–11 years. Courtship involves elaborate displays including 'sky-pointing' in which the bird points its bill at the sky with its wings spread. From January onwards, young birds display in communal 'dances'.

Breeding is largely concentrated at about 25 sites in the north-west of South Georgia and on Annenkov Island. The nest is a large pile of vegetation and soil with a depression in the centre. The single egg is laid in December and hatches in March after 75–83 day incubation. Chick spends winter on nest and fledges in November-January after an average of 278 days. If breeding is successful, an egg is laid in alternate years. The diet is mainly squid with some fish and crustaceans, caught within 1 m of the surface.

The only species at South Georgia that raises chicks predominantly during austral winter. Adults have huge feeding range and may travel > 10,000 km on single foraging trip but most trips short. The chick is usually fed every 2–3 days but it can fast on land for several weeks between meals.

VULNERABLE	
Breeding visitor, breeding adults are ashore in all months	
SG:	1,553 pairs (2004)
GP:	8,050 pairs
Length:	110–135 cm
Wingspan:	270–325 cm

Threats: Susceptible to human disturbance. South Georgia population declining rapidly (about 4% per annum since late 1990s), mainly through incidental mortality in longline fisheries.

WHERE TO SEE: Most colonies are in the north-west of the island with a few at the south-east and on Annenkov Island. Visitors may view them on Prion island.

*See taxonomic notes *page 188*.

juvenile
stage 1/8

immature
stage 3/8

immature
stage 4/8

subadult
stage 5/8

subadult
stage 6/8

adult
stage 7/8

1

ABOVE: A Wandering Albatross courts with the 'sky-pointing' display.
BELOW: A Wandering Albatross guards a young chick.

ABOVE: A Wandering Albatross adds to its nest, watched by its mate.
BELOW: A juvenile Wandering Albatross prepares for its first flight.

① Black-browed Albatross

Thalassarche melanophrys

DISTRIBUTION: Circumpolar breeding distribution, including Falkland Islands (centre of population), Heard, Macquarie, South Georgia, Crozet, Kerguelen, Antipodes and Campbell Islands, and several island groups in Chile. During the non-breeding period, most South Georgia birds migrate to the Benguela Current upwelling system off south-west Africa, a small proportion to the Patagonian Shelf or Australasia.

IDENTIFICATION: Small, black and white albatross with white head. Prominent black feathers on brow and around eye. Juveniles have darker bills than adults, with black tips, and variable grey collar. Underwing white with black border wider under the leading edge. Follows ships.

VOICE: Wailing, croaking, groaning and bill-vibrating calls used at colony and when competing for food at sea.

BEHAVIOUR: Colonies are on steep slopes or terraces usually with Tussock Grass. The nest is a pillar of soil and vegetation. Median age of first breeding is 10 years and breeds annually. Single egg laid in late October-early November. Incubation is 65–72 days and fledging is 110–125 days in late April-May. Adults from South Georgia feed mainly north of the colony and in subantarctic waters during incubation, switching to predominantly antarctic waters during chick-rearing.

ENDANGERED	
Breeding visitor	
SG:	75,500 pairs (2004)
GP:	600,000 pairs
Length:	80–96 cm
Wingspan:	210–240 cm

Threats: Susceptible to human disturbance. South Georgia population declining rapidly (about 3–4% per annum since early 1990s), mainly because of incidental mortality in longline and trawl fisheries, and to a lesser extent reduced abundance of Antarctic Krill, one of its main prey.

WHERE TO SEE: Nests in about 15 areas in north-west South Georgia, in the southeast at Annenkov, Cooper and Green Islands, Rumbolds Point and at Clerke Rocks. The largest colonies are in the Willis Islands group, and Bird, Annenkov and Cooper Islands.

Juveniles can be confused with juvenile Grey-headed Albatrosses. They are distinguished by a whiter head, a black eye-patch and black bill tip.

① Grey-headed Albatross

Thalassarche chrysostoma

DISTRIBUTION: Circumpolar breeding distribution, including Macquarie, South Georgia, Crozet, Kerguelen, Campbell and Prince Edward Islands, and in Chile at Islas Diego Ramirez and Ildefonso. In non-breeding season adults range very widely throughout Southern Ocean, mainly in the open ocean. Very common at sea around South Georgia.

IDENTIFICATION: Small, black and white albatross similar in size to Black-browed Albatross (*page 58*), with grey head. Diagnostic striking black and yellow bill, and grey head and neck. Immatures similar (see Black-browed Albatross *page 58* for differences). Follows ships.

VOICE: Wailing, croaking and throbbing calls used at colony.

BEHAVIOUR: Colonies are usually on cliff tops and ledges. The nest is a pillar of soil and vegetation. Median age of first breeding is 12 years. Breeds biennially if successful. Single egg laid in October, Incubation is 69–78 days and fledging is about 140 days in May-June. Adults from South Georgia feed in the Antarctic Polar Frontal Zone and as far south as the southern boundary of the Scotia Sea and west of the Antarctic Peninsula. South Georgia birds show much variation in migration strategies after breeding. Individuals may remain predominantly in the south-west Atlantic, travel as far as the south-west Indian Ocean or complete one or two circumpolar migrations between breeding attempts.

VULNERABLE	
Breeding visitor	
SG:	47,800 pairs
GP:	95,750 pairs
Length:	70–90 cm
Wingspan:	205–230 cm

Threats: Susceptible to human disturbance. South Georgia population declining at >2% per annum since the early 1990s. Much less commonly reported in fisheries bycatch than many other albatrosses; hence, population decline may also reflect long-term decline in food abundance.

WHERE TO SEE: Breeds in nine areas/islands in the north-west of South Georgia. The largest colonies are at the Willis group, Bird Island and Paryadin Peninsula.

① White-capped Albatross

Thalassarche steadi

NEAR THREATENED	
Vagrant*	
SG:	1*
GP:	97,000 pairs
Length:	90–100 cm
Wingspan:	210–260 cm
Threats: Potentially susceptible to human disturbance.	

DISTRIBUTION: The great majority breed on the Auckland Islands. Migrates mainly to waters off South Africa and Chile; also regular in south-west Atlantic off Uruguay.

IDENTIFICATION: Medium-sized, black and white albatross, superficially similar to Black-browed Albatross (*page 58*), with pale head and underparts but larger, with a narrower black border to underwing, and a much deeper, grey bill with a yellow tip. Diagnostic black mark below forewing where it meets the body. Cheeks and sides of the neck usually pale greyish contrasting with white crown and forehead to give white-capped appearance.

VOICE: Wailing, croaking, groaning and bill-clopping at colony. Croaking calls used when competing for food at sea.

BEHAVIOUR: Timing of breeding and other aspects of reproductive biology little known. White-capped Albatrosses were assumed to nest annually but recent research suggests many could be biennial. The single male in the mixed pair at South Georgia breeds several weeks earlier than conspecifics at the Auckland Islands.

NOTE: A single male (*left*), first seen in the 2002/03 season, has bred with a female Black-browed Albatross at Bird Island since summer 2007/08. Chicks were hatched in 2007/08, 2008/09 and 2009/10 and one fledged successfully in 2009/10.

② Salvin's Albatross

Thalassarche salvini

VULNERABLE	
Vagrant	
Length:	90–100 cm
Wingspan:	210–260 cm

IDENTIFICATION: Slightly smaller than White-capped Albatross and distinguished by pale grey head and dull yellowish bill. Grey-headed Albatross (*page 60*) has black and yellow bill, dark grey head and more black on underwing.

A single non-breeding bird captured and ringed at a Grey-headed Albatross colony on Bird Island in 1982 was recorded subsequently among four breeding pairs on Ile des Pingouins in the Crozet archipelago in 1986. The rest of this species breed on the Bounty Islands and the Western Chain of the Snares Islands, New Zealand.

① Light-mantled Albatross

Phoebetria palpebrata

NEAR THREATENED	
Breeding visitor	
SG:	5,000 pairs
GP:	20,500 pairs
Length:	78–90 cm
Wingspan:	200–220 cm

DISTRIBUTION: Circumpolar breeding distribution, including Heard, Macquarie, South Georgia, Crozet, Kerguelen, Antipodes, Auckland, Campbell and Prince Edward Islands. Non-breeding birds from South Georgia remain predominantly in subantarctic and Antarctic waters in the south Atlantic and south-west Indian Oceans.

IDENTIFICATION: Medium-sized, graceful albatross with grey body (not always distinct) and contrasting sooty brown head and wings. Long thin wings and wedge-shaped tail give a distinctive elegant silhouette. Bill black with diagnostic blue stripe on lower mandible. Broader rear half of white eye-ring visible at close quarters.

VOICE: Characteristic mournful, two-syllable call when displaying. A throaty, guttural call and bill-snapping used to defend nest.

A pair on their gliding display flight.

BEHAVIOUR: Nests singly or in small groups on cliff ledges around much of the coast. Pairs of birds perform tandem display flights, gliding to and fro along coastal cliffs. Birds on ledges display by extending head and neck vertically while calling to passing birds. Breeds biennially if successful. Very long breeding season for a summer-nesting species. Single egg laid in late October-early November. Incubation is 65–71 days and fledging is 141–170 days in June. Adults from South Georgia have longer foraging trips on average and feed further south than other albatrosses during chick-rearing, to the southern boundary of the Scotia Sea and occasionally into the marginal ice zone of the Weddell Sea.

② Sooty Albatross

Phoebetria fusca

ENDANGERED	
Vagrant	
Length:	84–89 cm
Wingspan:	203 cm

DISTRIBUTION: Nearest breeding populations are at Tristan da Cunha and Gough Island.

IDENTIFICATION: Uniform chocolate-brown albatross with long thin wings and wedge-shaped tail.

COMPARISON: Sooty Albatross is usually readily distinguished from Light-mantled Albatross by dark body and, at close range, by yellow (not purple) bill-line. There can be confusion with darker individuals of the Light-mantled Albatross but these show a contrasting black head. Dark and juvenile forms of the Southern Giant Petrel (*page 66*) have paler bills and are less graceful, being more heavily built with broader wings, thicker necks and shorter tails.

Southern Giant Petrel

Macronectes giganteus

Resident	
SG:	8,700 pairs
GP:	48,000 pairs

Length:	80–100 cm
Wingspan:	185–210 cm

Threats: Susceptible to human disturbance. Occasional nest failures result from fur seals squashing eggs or chicks. South Georgia population stable or increasing slowly.

DISTRIBUTION: Breeds in the Antarctic Continent, on most subantarctic islands and north to the Falkland Islands, Gough Island and islands in southern Argentina and Chile. South Georgia juveniles disperse widely in the Southern Ocean whereas most adults remain in the south-west Atlantic. Nests South Sandwich Islands.

IDENTIFICATION: One of two similar species of mainly grey–brown and white petrels. White colour morph occurs rarely (<1% of South Georgia population). Similar in size to Black-browed Albatross (*page 58*), but slightly hump-backed. In flight, it flaps more and is less graceful. Juveniles are glossy grey-black, gradually becoming lighter with age, particularly on head and neck. Follows ships.

VOICE: Range of gurgling, whinnying, neighing, growling and mewing calls used defensively and in display. Usually silent at sea except when competing for food.

BEHAVIOUR: Nests in small colonies. The nest is a pile of vegetation or gravel. A single egg is laid in early-mid November. Incubation is 55–66 days and fledging is 104–132 days in late April-May (six weeks later than Northern Giant Petrel). Males are common on beaches in midsummer where they compete for fur seal carrion. Thereafter feeding extends to waters around South Georgia and the Scotia Sea. Females have a more marine distribution throughout breeding. They feed mainly in Antarctic waters and to a limited extent on the southern Patagonian Shelf. Some birds present on land almost year-round.

Northern Giant Petrel

Macronectes halli

Resident	
SG:	17,500 pairs
GP:	38,000 pairs

Length:	80–100 cm
Wingspan:	185–210 cm

Threats: Susceptible to human disturbance. Occasional nest failures result from fur seals crushing eggs or chicks. South Georgia population increasing probably as a result of increased carrion availability following the increase of the Antarctic Fur Seal population.

DISTRIBUTION: Circumpolar on subantarctic islands, including New Zealand north to Chatham Islands. South Georgia juveniles disperse widely in the Southern Ocean whereas adults remain in the southwest Atlantic.

IDENTIFICATION: Very similar to Southern Giant Petrel (for differences *see opposite*) but there is no white morph.

VOICE: As Southern Giant Petrel.

BEHAVIOUR: As Southern Giant Petrel although breeding time differs. A single egg is laid in late September–early October, Incubation is 57–62 days and fledging is 106–120 days in mid-late March.

COMPARISON: At close quarters, the Southern Giant Petrel can readily be distinguished from Northern Giant Petrel by green rather than red tip to bill. Hybrids between male Southern and female Northern Giant Petrels, with bill tip of intermediate colour, are very rare (<0·1% of birds).

1 Cape Petrel

Daption capense

DISTRIBUTION: Circumpolar including Antarctic continent and islands, and most subantarctic island groups. At least part of most populations migrate north after breeding, in South Atlantic regularly to southern Brazil. Nests South Sandwich Islands.

IDENTIFICATION: Unmistakeable medium-sized, stocky petrel with checkered black and white upperparts and wings, black head and tail and white underwing with black leading and trailing edges.

Resident/Partial migrant	
SG:	10,000 pairs
GP:	1 million pairs

Length:	35–42 cm
Wingspan:	80–90 cm

Threats: Nests on ledges and in crevices, mainly in inaccessible sites, so low likelihood of human disturbance. Rats on mainland may take eggs or small chicks.

VOICE: Range of churring, cackling and clucking calls used defensively and in display. Usually silent at sea except when competing for food.

BEHAVIOUR: Nests in loose colonies on cliff ledges in scattered sites around the coast. Nest is a shallow scrape among pebbles. Single egg laid in November-early December. Incubation is 41–50 days and fledging is 45–57 days in March. Defends nest aggressively with wings lowered and tail raised, and will readily spit stomach oil. Follows ships.

2 Antarctic Petrel

Thalassoica antarctica

DISTRIBUTION: Antarctic coasts and associated islands; also some inland mountains. Disperses north in winter but rarely seen north of 50° S.

Non-breeding visitor, mainly in winter	
Length:	40–46 cm
Wingspan:	100–110 cm

IDENTIFICATION: Medium-sized petrel similar in size to Cape Petrel (*above*), with brown head, upperparts and upper wing, except obvious broad white wing and tail bars. Underparts white but with brown neck, brown leading and trailing edges to wing and tail tip. Follows ships, often circling several times at great speed and then moving on. A more powerful and faster flier than the Cape Petrel.

① Snow Petrel

Pagodroma nivea *

DISTRIBUTION: Circumpolar, mainly on Antarctic continent and islands, also islands of Scotia Arc north to Bouvetøya and South Georgia. Southerly populations disperse north in winter but mainly south of 60°S. Nests South Sandwich Islands.

IDENTIFICATION: Unmistakeable small to medium-sized, all-white petrel with black bill and eye.

Resident	
SG:	3,000 pairs
GP:	2 million pairs

Length:	30–40 cm
Wingspan:	75–95 cm

Threats: Inaccessible nesting sites suggest a very low likelihood of human disturbance. Rats on mainland may take eggs or small chicks. South Georgia population status unknown.

VOICE: Range of guttural staccato cawing, churring, clucking and screeching calls used defensively and in display. Males thought to have deeper calls than females.

BEHAVIOUR: Nests under boulders or in crevices on steep slopes and cliffs often high in mountains. Single egg laid in late Nov-early December. Incubation is 41–49 days and fledging is 42–54 days in March. Defends nest by spitting stomach oil. Occasionally inspects ships and field parties.

② Southern Fulmar

Fulmarus glacialoides

DISTRIBUTION: Antarctica, Antarctic Peninsula and associated island groups north to Bouvetoya and the South Sandwich Islands. After breeding disperses widely, including north to southern Brazil. Nests South Sandwich Islands.

Non-breeding visitor, seen particularly in early-mid summer	
Length:	45–50 cm
Wingspan:	114–120 cm

IDENTIFICATION: Medium-sized grey and white petrel with distinctive stiff-winged wingbeats interspersed with gliding. Large head and white forehead. White underwing with dark trailing edge and outer primaries. Bill has pinkish base, dark nasal tubes and tip. Follows ships.

*See taxonomic notes page 188.

The all-white Snowy Sheathbill can be confused initially but has quick, jerking wingbeats and short, rounded wings.

1

2

1 Kerguelen Petrel
Aphrodroma brevirostris *

Non-breeding visitor, particularly in late summer and autumn	
Length:	33–36 cm
Wingspan:	80–82 cm

DISTRIBUTION: Breeds on Marion, Crozet, Kerguelen and Gough. Ranges north to 40° S and south to Drake Passage.

IDENTIFICATION: Medium-sized petrel, uniformly dark, similar in size to Soft-plumaged Petrel (*below*), and smaller than Great-winged Petrel (*page 74*). With experience, can be distinguished from these species by short stout neck, more rounded head, pale leading edge to underwing in some birds. Very distinctive fast, 'towering ' flight, showing prominent silvery underwing flashes. It rises high above the sea, hangs briefly then drops down.

2 Soft-plumaged Petrel
Pterodroma mollis

Non-breeding visitor, particularly in late summer	
Length:	32–37 cm
Wingspan:	83–95 cm

DISTRIBUTION: Tristan da Cunha, Gough, Marion, Crozet, Kerguelen, Antipodes Islands and Tasmania. Very widespread in southern oceans, regularly to 45–50° S.

IDENTIFICATION: Medium-size petrel with grey upperparts, breast band and neck, and white underparts. Distinguished from Atlantic Petrel (*page 74*) by white chin and throat, dark breast band, white undertail coverts and more patterned underwing.

3 White-headed Petrel
Pterodroma lessonii

Vagrant	
Length:	40–46 cm
Wingspan:	109 cm

DISTRIBUTION: Crozet, Kerguelen, Macquarie, Auckland and Antipodes Islands, mainly dispersing northwards and especially into the Pacific

IDENTIFICATION: Large, robust petrel with distinctive white forehead, greyish crown, back and upper tail, and obvious black eye-patch. Underparts white with incomplete dusky collar and contrasting underwing dark greyish-black.

*See taxonomic notes *page 188*.

1 Atlantic Petrel

Pterodroma incerta

Vagrant	
Length:	38–40 cm
Wingspan:	97–100 cm

DISTRIBUTION: Tristan da Cunha and Gough, chiefly dispersing west into south and south-west Atlantic, mainly north of the Subtropical Convergence but occasionally to west and north of South Georgia in austral autumn.

IDENTIFICATION: Large, robust, long-winged petrel with uniform dark chocolate brown upperparts, underwings, neck, upper chest and tail, and sharp demarcation with white lower chest and belly.

2 Great-winged Petrel

Pterodroma macroptera

ENDANGERED	
Vagrant	
Length:	43 cm
Wingspan:	104 cm

DISTRIBUTION: Gough, Tristan da Cunha, Amsterdam, Crozet, Kerguelen and Prince Edward Islands, and islands off Western Australia; another subspecies (Grey-faced Petrel – *see taxonomic notes (page 188)*) is widespread in New Zealand. Ranges at sea from 27–50° S.

IDENTIFICATION: Large, uniformly dark gadfly petrel with short, stout black bill. On underwings, outer flight feathers with silvery wash. A good view shows a dark eye-patch and paler throat. Wings are long and narrow and tail is longish and slightly wedge-shaped.

3 Grey Petrel

Procellaria cinerea

NEAR THREATENED	
Occasional non-breeding visitor	
Length:	50 cm
Wingspan:	115–130 cm

DISTRIBUTION: Tristan da Cunha, Gough, Marion, Crozet, Kerguelen, Campbell, Antipodes Islands. Disperses widely at sea, south of 25° S.

IDENTIFICATION: A large petrel similar in size to White-chinned Petrel (*page 76*). It is heavy-bodied with long, narrow wings. The head, body and wings are ash-grey, darker on the face, and white underparts. It characteristic flight is effortless with long glides and shallow wingbeats.

White-chinned Petrel

Procellaria aequinoctialis

DISTRIBUTION: Circumpolar breeding distribution, including Falklands (very local), South Georgia, Prince Edward, Crozet, Kerguelen, Antipodes, Campbell and Auckland Islands. The majority of South Georgia adults spend the non-breeding period on the Patagonian Shelf, particularly off south-eastern Brazil and Uruguay and, less commonly, move in midwinter to the Humboldt Current region of western Chile.

IDENTIFICATION: Large, long-winged, stocky, dark petrel with greenish yellow bill. The white chin is variable and sometimes almost invisible. Follows ships.

VOICE: Loud chattering rattling and wheezy calls at colonies. Usually silent at sea.

BEHAVIOUR: Nests in burrows, usually between clumps of tall Tussock Grass. Single egg laid in mid November–early December. Incubation is 57–62 days and fledging is 87–106 days in April-early May. During the pre-laying exodus and incubation, adults from South Georgia feed on the Patagonian Shelf, but after chicks hatch, switch to waters predominantly in the Antarctic Polar Frontal Zone and south to the South Orkney Islands. Diet is cephalopods, fish and crustaceans, sometimes caught by diving.

VULNERABLE	
Breeding visitor	
SG:	900,000 pairs
GP:	1·5 million pairs

Length:	51–58 cm
Wingspan:	134–147 cm

Threats: Rats on mainland may take eggs and small chicks. Degradation of tussac grassland by Antarctic Fur Seals and Reindeer results in burrow collapse, reduced cover and presumably higher predation rates by Brown Skuas; hence, distribution may have changed in recent decades. South Georgia population declining at about 2% per annum, mainly because of high mortality in longline and trawl fisheries.

COMPARISON: Distinguished from large shearwaters which also have light underparts by darker underwing, dusky undertail coverts, darkish hood and, at close range, slender greenish-yellow bill.

Antarctic Prion
Pachyptila desolata

Breeding visitor	
SG:	22 million pairs
GP:	25 million pairs

Length:	25–27 cm
Wingspan:	61–66 cm

DISTRIBUTION: Circumpolar breeding distribution on subantarctic islands, including South Georgia, Crozet, Kerguelen, Macquarie, Heard; also south along Scotia Arc at South Sandwich, South Orkney and South Shetland Islands; formerly at a few sites on coastal east Antarctica; possibly still at Scott Island. Ranges very widely at sea, north to 35°S. Although widespread in Antarctic and subantarctic waters, adults from South Georgia feed mainly within a few hundred kilometres of the island during the breeding season, and spend the non-breeding period in subantarctic and subtropical waters. Nests South Sandwich Islands.

Threats: Rats on mainland may take eggs, small chicks and possibly adults. In addition, degradation of tussac by Antarctic Fur Seals and Reindeer results in burrow collapse, reduced cover and presumably higher predation rates by Brown Skuas. Hence, there will have been a change in distribution in recent decades.

IDENTIFICATION: Small petrel with blue-grey upperparts, a dark 'M' mark across the upperwings, and dark tip to the tail. Underparts white with a prominent grey patch on the side of the neck and breast. The head has a dark eyestripe and a pale patch above the eye.

VOICE: Loud dove-like cooing call at colony.

BEHAVIOUR: Nests in long burrows mainly in areas of tall tussac grassland but also extends into moss banks and lower vegetation at higher altitudes. A single egg is laid in December, Incubation is 44–46 days and fledging is 45–55 days in March. Diet is crustaceans, molluscs and small fish caught at the surface. Flocks often fly alongside ships with erratic, twisting flight.

 ## Fairy Prion
Pachyptila turtur

Breeding visitor	
SG:	1,000 pairs
GP:	2·5 million pairs

Length:	23–28 cm
Wingspan:	56–60 cm

DISTRIBUTION: In addition to small populations on Falkland Islands and South Georgia, breeds on subantarctic and subtropical islands of Indian Ocean, New Zealand and Tasmania. Non-breeding distribution mainly reflects northerly dispersal to 30°S.

Threats: Rats on mainland may take eggs, small chicks and possibly adults.

IDENTIFICATION: The smallest prion with blue-grey upperparts and dark 'M' mark on the upperwings. The dark tip to the tail is noticeably broad. Wings rather short and broad. Tail long and wedge-shaped. Head appears pale with indistinct eyestripe.

VOICE: Loud *poor pop per* call at colony.

BEHAVIOUR: Nests in rock crevices on boulder beaches at the base of steep cliffs. The single egg is laid in November. Incubation is 44–56 days and fledging is 43–56 days in late February-early March. Coastal distribution and can be seen close inshore during daylight, when Antarctic Prions are farther out.

Antarctic Prion can be distinguished from Slender-billed (*page 80*) and Fairy Prions by its darker face and upperwing markings and from Broad-billed Prion (*page 80*) by smaller head and much smaller, blue bill. Identification of prions to species is often very difficult or impossible, especially if the visibility is poor.

Fairy Prion can be distinguished from other prions by its smaller size, much paler face and less pronounced markings except broad tailband.

① Slender-billed or Thin-billed Prion

Pachyptila belcheri

Non-breeding visitor. A few remains have been found among prion corpses killed by skuas but breeding at South Georgia has never been proven.	
Length:	25–26 cm
Wingspan:	56 cm

DISTRIBUTION: Nearest, large, breeding population is in the Falkland Islands, where it is common at sea south and east to the Polar Front; otherwise breeds only at Crozet and Kerguelen. Non-breeding distribution poorly known but mainly disperses to subtropical waters.

IDENTIFICATION: Small petrel with blue-grey upperparts and (compared with other prions) relatively faint dark 'M' mark on the upperwings, a narrow black tip to tail and thin bill.

② Broad-billed Prion

Pachyptila vittata

Vagrant. All records at sea are to the north of South Georgia and usually in years of high sea surface temperatures.	
Length:	25–30 cm
Wingspan:	57–66 cm

DISTRIBUTION: Nearest, large breeding populations are on Tristan da Cunha and Gough Islands.

IDENTIFICATION: Small petrel with greyish upperparts and pronounced dark 'M' mark on the upperwings, and narrow black tip to tail. Disproportionally wide, dark bill. Extensive grey sides to breast.

③ Blue Petrel

Halobaena caerulea

Breeding visitor	
SG:	70,000 pairs
GP:	1·5 million pairs
Length:	26–32 cm
Wingspan:	62–71 cm

Threats: Rats on mainland may take eggs, small chicks and possibly adults. Degradation of tussac grassland by Antarctic Fur Seals and Reindeer results in burrow collapse, reduced cover and presumably higher predation rates by Brown Skuas, which has led to changes in distribution in recent decades.

DISTRIBUTION: South Georgia, Prince Edward, Marion, Crozet, Kerguelen and Macquarie islands, and in southern Chile. Adults from South Georgia travel long distances to the southern Scotia Sea to feed during the breeding season, and also usually spend the non-breeding period in or to the north of the marginal ice zone.

IDENTIFICATION: Small petrel with greyish blue upperparts and whitish below. It is readily distinguished from prions, which are of a similar size and have plumage of similar colours, by darker cap, dark area around eye, lack of eyestripe, mottled greyish-white forehead, black bill and especially by the distinctive white tip to tail. Follows ships.

VOICE: Loud dove-like cooing call at colony.

BEHAVIOUR: Nests in long burrows in areas of tall tussac grassland. Single egg laid in October, Incubation is 49–55 days and fledging is 43–60 days in late January-early February. Diet is crustaceans, cephalopods and small fish caught at the surface. Follows ships, often with prions.

Antarctic Prion
for comparison

Broad-billed
Prion can be
distinguished from
other prions by
larger size, much
larger bill and steep
forehead.

2

1

1

3

Note the white
tip to the tail of a
Blue Petrel.

1 Great Shearwater

Puffinus gravis *

Summer visitor	
Length:	43–51 cm
Wingspan:	100–138 cm

DISTRIBUTION: Breeds on Tristan da Cunha and Gough, with small numbers in the Falkland Islands. Winters mainly in north-west Atlantic, leaving South Atlantic around April, returning October.

IDENTIFICATION: A large shearwater with dark crown, greyish-brown upperparts, whitish collar and rump, and black tail. Underparts mostly white, but with diagnostic dark patches on belly and underwing.

2 Sooty Shearwater

Puffinus griseus *

NEAR THREATENED	
Summer visitor	
Length:	40–46 cm
Wingspan:	94–105 cm

DISTRIBUTION: Nearest large population is in the Falkland Islands; very large numbers breed at islands off southern Chile and in New Zealand region. All populations migrate to Northern Hemisphere in winter.

IDENTIFICATION: Medium-sized, brownish-black shearwater with distinctive silvery grey underwing patches. Very fast flight with quick wing beats, long glides and short arcs over the water.

3 Little Shearwater

Puffinus assimilis *

Vagrant. Most records at sea to north and west (Shag Rocks area) of South Georgia and usually in years of high sea surface temperatures.	
Length:	25–30 cm
Wingspan:	58–67 cm

DISTRIBUTION: Nearest large populations at Tristan da Cunha and Gough Islands; otherwise confined to St Paul Island and New Zealand region.

IDENTIFICATION: A small shearwater with greyish black upperparts, dark cap that extends to below eye, white underparts, and white underwings with narrow dark border.

See taxonomic notes page 188.

Wilson's Storm-petrel

Oceanites oceanicus

Breeding visitor	
SG:	600,000 pairs
GP:	6–15 million pairs

Length:	15–19 cm
Wingspan:	38–42 cm

Threats: Rats on mainland may take eggs, small chicks and possibly adults. South Georgia population status unknown.

DISTRIBUTION: Circumpolar breeding distribution in subantarctic, Antarctica, Falkland Islands and Tierra del Fuego. Distribution at sea from Antarctic to 30°N in Pacific and 60°N in Atlantic. However, most adults from South Georgia appear to winter no further north than subtropical waters and the Patagonian Shelf. Nests South Sandwich Islands.

IDENTIFICATION: Small, very dark storm-petrel with conspicuous white rump patch extending to lower flanks. Legs and feet black with distinctive yellow webs. Pale bar across upperwing.

VOICE: Range of chatters and peeps, including nasal, grating two syllable *aark-aark* or wheezing call and, less commonly, *aark-uh-ah-ah-uh-uh* at colony.

BEHAVIOUR: Nests in crevices in rocky scree and cliffs; also in moss banks and adjacent areas of sparse vegetation. Occasionally seen over land during daylight. Single egg laid in mid December–January. Incubation is 33–59 days and fledging is 46–97 days during late March-mid May. Feeds by pattering on the sea surface or dipping to seize small animals at the surface. Follows ships and associates with cetaceans.

② Black-bellied Storm-petrel

Fregetta tropica

Breeding visitor	
SG:	10,000 pairs
GP:	250,000 pairs

Length:	20 cm
Wingspan:	45–46 cm

Threats: Rats on mainland may take eggs, small chicks and potentially adults.

DISTRIBUTION: Circumpolar breeding distribution. Mainly recorded south of the Antarctic Polar Front in breeding season. Nests South Sandwich Islands.

IDENTIFICATION: Large storm-petrel with black head, neck and upperparts. Rump, centre of underwings and flanks white; belly white with variable black central stripe.

VOICE: High pitched, whistling *huuuuu*, or lower, repeated *pee-ee-pip-pip*.

BEHAVIOUR: Nests in burrows in moss banks, grassy slopes and among stable boulder scree. A local breeder, it is recorded at Bird Island and a few sites on mainland South Georgia. Single egg laid in mid December-January. Incubation is 35–44 days and fledging is 65–71 days in April. Feeds by pattering on the sea surface or dipping to seize small fish and crustaceans.

COMPARISON: White on belly distinguishes Black-bellied Storm-petrel from Wilson's Storm-petrel and black stripe on belly distinguishes it from most White-bellied Storm-petrels, although the stripe can be very narrow.

③ Grey-backed Storm-petrel

Garrodia nereis

Breeding visitor	
SG:	<100 pairs
GP:	100,000 pairs

Length:	16–19 cm
Wingspan:	39 cm

Threats: Rats on mainland may take eggs, small chicks and possibly adults. South Georgia population status unknown.

DISTRIBUTION: Falkland Islands and subantarctic Islands. Mainly seen within a few hundred km of breeding islands during summer. Adults probably winter north of the Antarctic Polar Front.

IDENTIFICATION: A small storm petrel with mainly ashy-grey upperparts. Black head, neck, upper breast and broad leading edge of underwings. Belly and centre of underwings are white. Long, slender black legs.

VOICE: Low, regular, cricket-like wheezy chirp or croak.

BEHAVIOUR: Nests in burrows in dense tussac. Single egg laid in December. Incubation is about 45 days. Fledging, period unknown, is in March. Often seen feeding around floating kelp and other material.

South Georgia Diving-petrel

Pelecanoides georgicus

Breeding visitor	
SG:	2 million pairs
GP:	7 million pairs
Length:	18–22 cm
Wingspan:	37–43 cm
Threats: Rats on mainland take eggs, small chicks and possibly adults.	

DISTRIBUTION: Circumpolar breeding distribution on subantarctic islands, including South Georgia, Crozet, Kerguelen, Prince Edward, Heard and Auckland Islands. Also Codfish Island, New Zealand. During the non-breeding period, most birds probably remain in the vicinity of the islands with a few dispersing south in the Scotia Sea or north to the Antarctic Polar Frontal Zone.

IDENTIFICATION: Small, stocky petrel with dark brown to black upperparts, and white underparts, black bill and blue legs. Characteristic whirring, auk-like flight close to sea surface.

VOICE: Squeaking call at colony.

BEHAVIOUR: Nests in long burrows in fine scree, sometimes at considerable altitude. Shorter-lived and breeds for first time at much younger age than other petrels. Single egg laid in December. Incubation is 44–52 days and fledging is 43–60 days in March. Feeds on krill, cephalopods and fish. Adults from South Georgia feed mainly within a few hundred km of the island during the breeding season.

② Common Diving-petrel

Pelecanoides urinatrix *

Breeding visitor	
SG:	3·8 million pairs
GP:	8 million pairs
Length:	20–25 cm
Wingspan:	37–46 cm
Threats: Rats on mainland take eggs, small chicks and possibly adults. Degradation of tussac by Antarctic Fur Seals and Reindeer results in burrow collapse, reduced cover and presumably higher predation rates by Brown Skuas. Hence, there has been a change in distribution in recent decades.	

DISTRIBUTION: Circumpolar breeding distribution on most subantarctic islands, with other subspecies on islands around mainland New Zealand and south-east Australia, Tristan da Cunha group and Falkland Islands. Adults from South Georgia feed mainly within a few hundred kilometres of the island throughout the year, although a small proportion migrate to further south in the Scotia Sea during the non-breeding period.

IDENTIFICATION: Small, stocky petrel with dark brown to black upperparts, and white underparts, black bill and blue legs. Characteristic whirring, auk-like flight close to sea surface.

VOICE: Loud, harsh *kooo-ah* and *kuaka-did-a-did* call at colony.

BEHAVIOUR: Nests in steep seaward-facing tussac slopes. Shorter-lived and breeds for first time at much younger age than other petrels. Single egg laid in October-early November. Incubation is 53 days and fledging is 45–59 days in February (breeding is >1 month earlier than South Georgia Diving-petrel. Feeds mainly on marine crustaceans.

*See taxonomic notes *page 188.*

COMPARISON: Diving-petrels cannot usually be separated reliably at sea, except under optimum conditions. The South Georgia Diving-petrel is smaller, has a broader white trailing edge to the secondaries, whiter sides to the neck and is paler under the wings and on the sides. In the hand it can be distinguished easily by a black line on the rear of the tarsus (*inset*).

① Imperial Shag

*Phalacrocorax atriceps**

DISTRIBUTION: Antarctic Peninsula, southern South America, Falkland Islands. Nests South Sandwich Islands.

IDENTIFICATION: The only cormorant recorded at South Georgia. The sexes are similar but males are generally larger. Breeding adults are pied, with the black upperparts exhibiting blue, violet and green iridescence. Underparts and a narrow patch on the wing coverts are white. Bill thin and dark grey, with an orange cauliflower-like nasal caruncle at the base. Legs and webbed feet are pink. The eye-ring is bright blue and the head is crowned by an erectile crest. Non-breeders lack the crest and have duller plumage and bare parts. In juvenile birds, the parts that are black in adults are dull brown, soft parts are duller and the crest is lacking.

VOICE: Males honk and females hiss when threatened.

BEHAVIOUR: Breeds among tussac on cliff ledges or steep slopes overlooking the sea.
Lays 2–3 greyish eggs in November or December. Incubation is around 30 days and fledging is about 65 days. Unlike other cormorants, never spreads wings when perched. It is believed this is because it has more waterproof feathers than other cormorants, as an adaptation to a cold environment. Feeds on or close to sea bed, which restricts it to inshore waters throughout the year. Sexual segregation of foraging, with males foraging later in the day, further from colony and diving deeper. Dives, up to 110 m deep, preceded by a leap clear of the water. Food mainly nototheniid fish, polychaete worms and octopods.

Resident	
SG:	10,300 pairs
GP:	170,000–700,000 pairs

Length:	72–75 cm
Wingspan:	122–126 cm

Threats: None known at South Georgia; vulnerable to gill nets in its South American range.

WHERE TO SEE: Widely distributed around South Georgia. Likely to be seen in nesting colonies on cliffs or swimming in and flying over inshore waters.

Imperial Shag in non-breeding plumage.

*See taxonomic notes *page 188*.

Cocoi Heron

Ardea cocoi

Vagrant	
Length:	120 cm
Wingspan:	190–230 cm

DISTRIBUTION: Southern South America, vagrant to Falkland Islands.

IDENTIFICATION: A large heron, similar to Grey Heron of Eurasia, with back and wings grey, latter with black shoulder patch; neck and underparts white (with black belly), cap black; bill yellow; legs dark. In flight primaries dark, contrasting with rest of wing. Juvenile has dark greenish bill and generally dusky (rather than white) on neck and underparts.

Great Egret

Ardea alba*

Vagrant	
Length:	85–105 cm
Wingspan:	140–170 cm

DISTRIBUTION: Widespread species globally. Likely origin South America.

IDENTIFICATION: A large heron, with a long, sinuous neck. Plumage entirely white and legs black. Slender yellow bill, iris and facial skin.

Cattle Egret

Bubulcus ibis*

Regular (most years) non-breeding visitor	
Length:	50–56 cm
Wingspan:	90–96 cm

DISTRIBUTION: A global species, likely origin of visitors to South Georgia is South America.

IDENTIFICATION: A small, relatively stocky heron often seen in flocks. In non-breeding adults and juveniles, plumage is completely white. The robust bill, iris and facial skin around the bill and eye are pale yellow, and the legs and feet are yellowish (greyish-green in juveniles). It is more terrestrial than other species of egret.

Perched on an elephant seal.

Snowy Egret

Egretta thula

Vagrant	
Length:	56–66 cm
Wingspan:	95–100 cm

DISTRIBUTION: Widespread in wetlands of southern North America and throughout South America. Likely origin South America.

IDENTIFICATION: A small, slender heron. Plumage white, bill dark, with facial skin and iris yellow. Feet and back of legs are yellow, with front of legs black.

See taxonomic notes page 188.

1

2

3

4

① South Georgia Pintail

Anas georgica*

Resident	
SG:	6,000 pairs
GP:	No figures
Length:	39–45 cm
Wingspan:	65–70 cm

DISTRIBUTION: Falkland Islands and southern South America. South Georgia population is an endemic species.

IDENTIFICATION: Medium-sized duck with pointed tail. Brown body with yellow on the sides of the bill. Sexes are similar but males slightly larger with lemon yellow rather than dull yellow on bill. The belly varies between brown and white. Legs are olive-green, occasionally dappled yellow in males. Speculum brown with buff border, brighter in males and often with a hint of green.

Threats: Small population size and vulnerability to nest predation by rats. Pintails are sometimes predated by skuas and occasionally by Leopard Seals.

WHERE TO SEE: Found individually or in small groups all round the coast, rarely venturing far inland. Up to 80 may occur on favoured bathing pools.

VOICE: A wheezy chirp in males, and a deeper quack or rasp in females.

BEHAVIOUR: Forms flocks when not nesting. Usually nests off the ground in tussac. Up to five eggs laid between November and February and incubated by female. Incubation is 24–28 days but the fledging period is unknown. Ducklings normally remain hidden in dense vegetation and on small pools in daylight. Female defends the brood with a distraction display in which she runs from brood while flapping her wings conspicuously. A full post-breeding moult, in which the birds become flightless, occurs in January-April, during which time some or most birds are strictly nocturnal, and the species seems to disappear. Feeds mostly in the intertidal zone and in streams on leaves, seeds and crustaceans. Scavenges on seal carcasses.

*See taxonomic notes *page 188*.

COMPARISON: The pintail is larger than the much rarer Speckled Teal (*page 94*), with longer neck and tail, more uniformly brown, and with breast, flanks and under tail coverts clearly spotted. It is also far more confiding: if you are close enough to see a duck without binoculars, almost certainly it will be a South Georgia Pintail.

 Speckled Teal

Anas flavirostris

DISTRIBUTION: Widespread in Falklands and southern South America; an immigrant to South Georgia since the 1950s, it has never been common there. Small flocks have been encountered near Grytviken and on the Greene Peninsula, but less frequently in recent years.

IDENTIFICATION: A small and slim brown duck, with smoky grey/brown sides, light belly, yellow on the sides of the bill and olive legs. Sexes similar. Superficially similar to the South Georgia Pintail (*page 92*).

VOICE: Quite similar to South Georgia Pintail. Loud, high-pitched *priip* display whistle most common in male. Quack or rasping call in females.

BEHAVIOUR: A fast-flying duck, this species usually mixes with the larger and less agile South Georgia Pintail. It is rarely found in the intertidal zone except in winter when all fresh water is frozen.

Resident	
SG:	Fewer than 20 pairs.
Population probably maintained by immigration from Falklands/ southern South America, where abundant.	
GP:	No figures
Length:	37–43 cm
Wingspan:	63–69 cm

Threats: It is likely to be vulnerable to rat predation of its young and may no longer breed regularly on South Georgia.

WHERE TO SEE: Encountered in ones and twos almost anywhere near the coast, but never common. Less marine than the South Georgia Pintail.

Chiloe Wigeon

Anas sibilatrix

DISTRIBUTION: South America and Falkland Islands.

IDENTIFICATION: Head and neck are black except for white forehead and face. The breast is finely barred black and white and the flanks are orange. The back, wings and tail are black with white streaks and a white rump. The female is duller than the male.

Vagrant	
Length:	48–53 cm
Wingspan:	70–75 cm

Turkey Vulture

Cathartes aura *

Vagrant	
Length:	66–71 cm
Wingspan:	157–170 cm

DISTRIBUTION: Found throughout North and South America and in the Falkland Islands.

IDENTIFICATION: A large bird of prey, with broad wings and well-separated primaries that form 'fingers'. Plumage largely black, though undersides of flight and tail feathers are paler grey. Bare, wrinkled skin of head and legs are a dull red or pink; bill whitish. Soars effortlessly on updraughts with wings in a shallow V and tilting from side to side.

 Peregrine

Falco peregrinus *

Vagrant	
Length:	28–50 cm
Wingspan:	80–120 cm

DISTRIBUTION: A pan-global species with a likely origin in southern South America or Falkland Islands. Visitors to South Georgia are probably ship-assisted.

IDENTIFICATION: A large, powerful falcon whose pointed, swept-back wings and stocky body give an anchor-like flight silhouette. Adult upperparts bluish grey with darker barring on the tail, underparts white with fine black barring. Black hood on head with characteristic dark moustachial stripe extending down white throat. Legs, iris, orbital ring and cere yellow. In immature birds dark areas of adults are brown and undersides are streaked rather than barred, with soft parts greyish.

See taxonomic notes page 188.

① Snowy Sheathbill
Chionis albus

Resident/partial migrant	
SG:	2,000 pairs
GP:	10,000 pairs

Length:	31–41 cm
Wingspan:	74–84 cm

Threats: Pollutants may represent a threat within the wintering range.

DISTRIBUTION: Breeds from South Georgia to South Sandwich, South Orkney and South Shetland Islands and Antarctic Peninsula to 65°S. Many birds migrate north to winter in Falkland Islands and south-east South America, associating particularly with seabird and seal colonies, and often in fishing harbours in Argentina. Nests South Sandwich Islands.

IDENTIFICATION: Plump, small-headed, bantam-sized bird. Plumage white. Legs grey and feet not webbed. The laterally flattened, bullet-profiled bill is coloured horn with an indistinct black edging. Beady black eyes set in bare and pink facial skin with grotesque caruncles. Walks briskly on strong legs, bobbing head in pigeon-like manner. In flight, wings short and rounded. Long neck and short tail contribute to front-heavy appearance.

VOICE: Typically silent but utters a number of grunting calls. The old nickname of 'mutt' is onomatopoeic.

BEHAVIOUR: Seen around penguin and seal colonies and on rocky shores. Lays 1–4 whitish eggs in an untidy nest of pebbles, bones and other available debris sited within a rock cavity. Incubation is about 30 days and fledging about 55 days. Omnivorous, feeding on carrion, eggs, small chicks, algae, invertebrates and human refuse. Sheathbills also steal food (krill) from penguins by flying at adults when they are feeding chicks so the food is spilt. Defend themselves by spraying foetid faeces. Very confiding and inquisitive.

Brown Skua
Stercorarius antarcticus *

Breeding visitor	
SG:	2,000 pairs
GP:	8,000 pairs

Length:	52–64 cm
Wingspan:	125–160 cm

Threats: Susceptible to human disturbance. Occasional nest failures may result from seals squashing eggs or chicks, and possibly predation of small chicks by Brown Rats. Population has increased at Bird Island and probably at other sites because of increased carrion from the recovering Antarctic Fur Seal population.

DISTRIBUTION: Circumpolar breeding distribution, including all subantarctic island groups, Antarctic Peninsula and associated island groups south to 65°S, north to South Georgia (ssp. *lonnbergi*); also Falkland Islands and south-east Argentina (ssp. *antarcticus*) and Tristan da Cunha (ssp. *hamiltoni*). Nests South Sandwich Islands.

IDENTIFICATION: A heavily-built, brown bird, with pale streaks and blotches, often with a darker cap and wings. Broad wings with conspicuous white flashes at base of primaries. Black bill and legs. Juveniles darker and more uniform in colour than adults.

VOICE: Range of raucous, guttural calls used in display and when competing for food. Characteristic long call of several notes, with initial rise in pitch and volume, uttered with wings outstretched on ground or in flight.

BEHAVIOUR: Breeds in loose colonies. Nest is a scrape sometimes with a scant lining of vegetation. A clutch of 1–2 eggs (usually 2) is laid in late November-early December. Incubation is 28–32 days and fledging is 40–50 days in late February-March. Breeding pairs are famous for the violent 'dive-bombing' attacks on humans and seals approaching the nest. Very common on beaches, particularly in midsummer when adults compete for fur seal placentas and carrion. Diet includes fish, burrow-nesting seabirds caught mainly at night, penguin eggs and chicks. Adults with eggs or chicks rarely feed at sea. During non-breeding period, adults disperse to deep, oceanic water on the edge of the Patagonian Shelf and in the Argentine Basin.

② South Polar Skua
Stercorarius maccormicki

Occasional non-breeding visitor	
Length:	50–55 cm
Wingspan:	120–160 cm

DISTRIBUTION: In recent years, most commonly seen in late summer (presumably migrants en route to North Atlantic wintering grounds). Nearest breeding populations in the South Orkney Islands (although few birds), South Shetland Islands and Antarctic Peninsula region (circumpolar on Antarctic Continent).

IDENTIFICATION: Similar to the Brown Skua (*above*) but smaller and less heavily-built. Plumage is variable with dark, pale and intermediate colour morphs. Pale morph has diagnostic pale head and underparts that contrast with dark wings and upperparts. Intermediate morph less distinctive, Dark morph can be distinguished with care from Brown Skua by overall slighter build, and shorter and more slender bill.

*See taxonomic notes page 188.

1

1

2 pale morph

2 pale morph

2 dark morph

Kelp Gull
Larus dominicanus

Resident	
SG:	2,000 pairs
GP:	1·6–2·1 million pairs
Length:	54–65 cm
Wingspan:	128–142 cm
Threats: None.	

DISTRIBUTION: Subantarctic islands and Antarctic Peninsula to 68°S. South America north to Ecuador and Brazil; southern Africa, New Zealand and south-east Australia. Nests South Sandwich Islands.

IDENTIFICATION: The only gull breeding on South Georgia. Adults unmistakable, with white underparts, head, rump and tail; back and upper-wings mostly black. Upperwings have broad white band along trailing edge and primaries tipped white, forming a row of four white 'mirrors' in the wing when it is folded. Bill yellow with red spot near the tip of the lower mandible. Eye pale yellow with red orbital ring, and legs greyish-green. During winter the head and neck are streaked brown. Immature is heavily streaked and scaled with buff brown, with dark brown primaries, secondaries and tail feathers, superficially resembling Brown Skua (*page 100*) but paler and lacking white wing-flashes. Bill and eye dark. Legs greyish. Transition to adult plumage takes four years. Body and iris become paler, wing and back feathers become darker and bill colouration becomes brighter.

VOICE: Alarm calls are a clipped *kok-kok-kok* or a strident *kyow*. Territorial long-call a series of kyow calls, the first one extended and followed by up to 10 clipped ones. Contact call a plaintive *meeu*. Chick begging call a whistling *shi-ooo*.

BEHAVIOUR: Some Kelp Gulls disperse northwards outside the breeding season. Breeding takes place between September and January. Birds breed in coastal sites as single pairs or in small colonies. Nest is an untidy pile of vegetation in which 1–3 greenish or brownish eggs with black specking are laid in late November. Incubation is 24–30 days and fledging is 49 days in late January and early February. Diet is largely limpets and other intertidal invertebrates, but gulls also scavenge carrion, refuse and fishery waste and prey on eggs and small chicks of other birds.

 # Dolphin Gull
Leucophaeus scoresbii

Vagrant	
Length:	40–46 cm
Wingspan:	104–110 cm

DISTRIBUTION: Resident in southern South America and Falkland Islands.

IDENTIFICATION: Medium sized gull. Adults have dusky grey wash to head and body, blackish upperwings with white trailing edge, white tail and bright red bill, legs and eye-ring. Non-breeders often show a darker hood. Juveniles mostly uniform dark brown with paler belly, a white trailing edge to the wing and greyish bare parts. Adult plumage acquired by third year.

Antarctic Tern
Sterna vittata

Breeding visitor	
SG:	2,500 pairs
GP:	65,000–75,000 pairs
Length:	32–40 cm
Wingspan:	74–79 cm

Threats: Particularly susceptible to human disturbance, so visitors should avoid walking through, or even closely approaching, breeding colonies.

DISTRIBUTION: Breeds throughout subantarctic islands (north to Tristan da Cunha) and on Antarctic Peninsula to 68°S. Ranges north to South America and South Africa outside breeding season. Nests South Sandwich Islands.

IDENTIFICATION: The only tern breeding at South Georgia. Breeding adult has uniformly grey body. Cheek stripe, trailing edge to wing, rump and tail are white and the cap is matt black. Flight feathers are largely opaque. Tail is deeply forked but streamers relatively short, and are a few centimetres shorter than the wingtips when perched. The dagger-shaped bill, short legs and webbed feet are blood red. Non-breeding birds have a pale forehead and duller bill and legs. Juveniles have dark streaked cap, heavily barred upperparts and black legs and bill (*inset*). Barring lost in immature plumage and adult plumage is attained at three years.

VOICE: Alarm call is a shrill *kik-kik-kriah* and display call a loud, repeated *chit-chit-chit-chirr*.

BEHAVIOUR: Breeds in colonies. The 1–2 green or brown eggs with black speckling are laid in November, in a scrape lined with pebbles, shells or vegetation. Incubation is 23 days and fledging is 27 days. Flight is fast and buoyant. Members of a colony attack human intruders, sometimes striking with their bill. Diet is largely small fish and crustaceans. On locating prey a tern hovers up to about 10 m before plunge-diving or dipping to capture.

COMPARISON: Confusion with Arctic Tern in South Georgia waters only likely to occur during non-breeding period when Antarctic Tern is also in non-breeding plumage. The Arctic Tern can be distinguished by the shorter bill and legs, longer tail streamers with dark outer webs and translucent flight feathers.

 Arctic Tern
Sterna paradisaea

Vagrant (although probably more regular than confirmed records suggest)	
Length:	33–35 cm
Wingspan:	75–85 cm

DISTRIBUTION: Breeds in Arctic and temperate regions throughout the northern hemisphere and migrates to the Southern Ocean for austral summer.

IDENTIFICATION: Non-breeding adults are overall pale grey, with white trailing edge to wing and white tail. Head mostly pale grey and white, with black crescent extending over the hind crown and nape from one eye to the other forming a mask. Short bill and legs dark. Immatures have a dusky bar along the front of the wing.

Arctic Tern has translucent flight feathers.

2nb

1b

1j

1b

2nb

1 White-rumped Sandpiper

Calidris fuscicollis

Regular visitor	
Length:	15–17 cm
Wingspan:	40–45 cm

DISTRIBUTION: Breeds in coastal tundra of arctic North America and winters in southern South America, below the equator and east of the Andes.

IDENTIFICATION: Small, attenuated wader with horizontal posture and long wings that extend beyond the tail when folded. Feathers of upperparts pale grey with darker central streak. Pale underparts with grey streaking on breast and flanks. Juveniles more scaly above. Diagnostic white rump clearly visible in flight.

2 Pectoral Sandpiper

Calidris melanotos

Vagrant	
Length:	19–23 cm
Wingspan:	42–49 cm

DISTRIBUTION: Breeds in coastal tundra of Arctic America. Winters in South America down to Uruguay and northern Argentina.

IDENTIFICATION: A medium sized, stocky wader. Feathers of head, breast and upperparts brown fringed with buff, creating scaly/streaked appearance (particularly in juveniles). White underparts and clearly demarcated streaking on breast form pectoral band from which the species takes its name. Bill dark and slightly drooping and legs dull yellow. Rump has broad dark central band. Plain appearance in flight with inconspicuous whitish wingbar.

COMPARISON: Similar Baird's Sandpiper *Calidris bairdii*, an accidental, can be distinguished by dark rump, unstreaked flanks and wings extending beyond the tail.

① South Georgia Pipit

Anthus antarcticus

DISTRIBUTION: Endemic to South Georgia.

IDENTIFICATION: The only passerine breeding on South Georgia. Plumage buff or ochre-brown heavily streaked with black. Prominent dark malar stripe; wing-bar and outer tail feathers off-white. Bill greyish brown, legs pale flesh brown, with long hind-claw.

Similar to Correndera Pipit *A. correndera* of the Falkland Islands, which is smaller and duller, less heavily streaked and has pale 'braces' on the back. Although never recorded in South Georgia it is a possible vagrant.

VOICE: Song, delivered in flight, a monotonous repetition of soft, high-pitched sequences. Alarm call when flushed is short and soft *schwip*.

NEAR THREATENED	
Resident	
SG:	3,000 pairs

Length:	16·5 cm
Wingspan:	134–147 cm

Threats: Nests predated by rats whose spread following the recession of glaciers threatens the remaining mainland habitats. Accidental introduction of rats to offshore islands is a perpetual risk. The planned eradication of rats from South Georgia will safeguard existing populations and allow expansion of range and population.

BEHAVIOUR: Now confined to about 20 rat-free offshore islands and areas of the southern mainland that are isolated from rat invasion by glaciers. Breeds February in low-altitude tussac habitat. Nest cup constructed of vegetation, lined with feathers, and sited under overhanging Tussock Grass. 3–5 brownish speckled eggs are laid in September and October. Incubation and fledging periods not known. Productivity high (several broods each year) but overwinter survival is low. Winters on ice-free shorelines. Diet includes insects and small crustaceans.

VAGRANT SPECIES: Species which have been recorded at South Georgia 2 to 20 times.

Barn Swallow

Hirundo rustica *

Length:	17–19cm
Wingspan:	32–34cm

DISTRIBUTION: Breeds in temperate North America (and Eurasia) and migrates to winter in South America, south to Tierra del Fuego and occasionally the Falkland Islands (and sub-Saharan Africa). Likely origin South America.

IDENTIFICATION: A small swallow with deeply forked tail, dark metallic blue upperparts, pale buffish underparts and rusty red throat (bordered by dark partial breastband) and forehead.

Chilean Swallow

Tachycineta leucopyga *

Length:	12–13cm
Wingspan:	26–29cm

DISTRIBUTION: Breeds in southern South America, migrating north in austral winter to northern Argentina and southern Brazil; annual visitor to Falkland Islands where it has bred once.

IDENTIFICATION: A small swallow with deep metallic-blue upperparts contrasting with obvious white rump and underparts. Tail is slightly forked and lacks streamers. All bare parts black.

NOTE: It is expected that new species of vagrants and accidentals will continue to be added to the list of South Georgia birds. Please inform the SGHT at the address shown on page 200.

*See taxonomic notes *page 188.*

ACCIDENTAL SPECIES: Species which have been recorded at South Georgia once only.

See taxonomic notes *page 188*

Barn Owl	*Tyto alba*
Black-necked Swan	*Cygnus melanocoryphus*
Blue-winged Teal	*Anas discors*
Purple Gallinule	*Porphyrio martinica*
Allen's Gallinule	*Porphyrio alleni*
Rufous-chested Plover	*Charadrius modestus*
Solitary Sandpiper	*Tringa solitaria*
Spotted Sandpiper	*Actitis macularius*
Little Stint	*Calidris minuta*
Baird's Sandpiper	*Calidris bairdii*
Wilson's Phalarope	*Phalaropus tricolor*
Long-tailed Skua	*Stercorarius longicaudus*
Franklin's Gull	*Leucophaeus pipixcan*
Dark-faced Ground-tyrant	*Muscisaxicola maclovianus*
Eastern Kingbird	*Tyrannus tyrannus*
Long-tailed Meadowlark	*Sturnella loyca*
Grey-flanked Cinclodes	*Cinclodes oustaleti*

INTRODUCED SPECIES:

Upland Goose	*Chloephaga picta*

SHIP-ASSISTED SPECIES:

Eared Dove	*Zenaida auricularia*
Upland Goose	*Chloephaga picta*
House Sparrow	*Passer domesticus*

UNCONFIRMED SIGHTINGS IN SG&SSI AREA:

see page 50

Northern Royal Albatross	*Diomedea sanfordi*
Manx Shearwater	*Puffinus puffinus*
Mottled Petrel	*Pterodroma inexpectata*
White-bellied Storm-petrel	*Fregetta grallaria*
Red Knot	*Calidris canutus*
Brown-headed Gull	*Chroicocephalus maculipennis*

Species recorded in the South Atlantic sector of the Southern Ocean at latitudes south of South Georgia but yet to be recorded at South Georgia

Leach's Storm-petrel	*Oceanodroma leucorhoa*
Pomarine Skua	*Stercorarius pomarinus*
Arctic Skua	*Stercorarius parasiticus*
Grey (Red) Phalarope	*Phalaropus fulicarius*
Upland Sandpiper	*Bartramia longicauda*
Least Sandpiper	*Calidris minutilla*
South American Snipe	*Gallinago paraguaiae*
White-crested Elaenia	*Elaenia albiceps*

SEALS

True seals swim with their hindflippers which are spread like a fish tail and swung from side to side. They move over land on their bellies with an ungainly, bouncing, 'caterpillar' action.

Eared seals have small external 'ears' (actually flaps of skin) which true seals lack. They swim by beating their long foreflippers up and down and they move rapidly on land by turning their hindflippers forward and lifting their bodies off the ground. Males are substantially larger than females.

The Weddell Seal's 'friendly' expression.

A Southern Elephant Seal bull flicks sand over its back.

ABOVE LEFT: A Leopard Seal emerges through the kelp.

ABOVE RIGHT: A Leopard Seal thrashes a penguin.

RIGHT: An Antarctic Fur Seal is curious about human divers.

1 Antarctic Fur Seal
Arctocephalus gazella

DISTRIBUTION: Scotia Sea, including the South Sandwich, South Orkney and South Shetland Islands, with smaller populations on Bouvet, Kerguelen and Macquarie Islands.

IDENTIFICATION: The only 'eared' seal on South Georgia (apart from the very rarely occurring Subantarctic Fur Seal, *page 117*), it is immediately recognisable by the way it 'stands up', tucking the hindflippers under the body and 'walking' on its foreflippers.

Pups are black but juveniles and adult cows are grey/brown above and silvery-white below. Adult bulls are grey/brown all over. One seal in 1,000 is cream-coloured due to a recessive gene (*below*).

VOICE: Bulls 'huff' aggressively. Cows and pups have a loud high-pitched wail, almost human-like, with which they locate each other on a crowded beach. In December, South Georgia resounds to their plaintive voices. Pups growl at each other and at humans who mistakenly think they are cute enough to stroke!

BEHAVIOUR: Antarctic Fur Seals move surprisingly fast on land, and are exquisite acrobats in the water, often porpoising over long distances. They are famed for their aggression, especially during the breeding season, when bulls fight ferociously in defence of harems and attack intruding humans. The bulls come ashore in November and set up territories. Cows arrive and gather in dense colonies where bulls form them into harems of up to 20. They give birth from late November to early January, the peak being about 7–10 December. Unlike the true seals, fur seals have a long, four-month, lactation period. During this time cows leave their pups for several days at a time while they forage at sea.

Fur seals feed mainly on krill but also eat fish and occasionally kill and eat penguins. It is possible that the explosion in their population in the second half of the 20th century was partly due to the removal of competition from the krill-eating whales.

Resident	
SG:	>3 million 98 per cent of the species' global population breeds on South Georgia.
GP:	Low millions, having recovered from near extinction in the 19th century.

Length (male):	1·8–2·0 m
Length (female):	1·2 m
Weight (male):	80–90 kg
Weight (female):	30–50 kg

Threats: Once hunted for the very thick underfur that provides insulation. Now protected and very abundant. A few are entangled and may be killed in discarded fishing gear.

WHERE TO SEE: Widespread in the north-west and along most of the northern coast. An isolated breeding colony occurs at Cooper Bay in the south-east but the spread of seals from the north is rapidly closing the gap. Fur seals can also be seen in the open seas around South Georgia.

A rare 'blond' fur seal.

Conspicuous ears.

1m

1f

pup

FUR SEALS

ABOVE: Antarctic Fur Seal bulls guard territories with 'harems' of cows on a crowded breeding beach. Any intruding bull, or human, will be attacked.
BELOW: The breeding beach is fully occupied and extra bulls line the shallows just offshore. More seals find their way into the tussac behind the beach.

The contrasting 'bib' and the hairy crest of a bull Subantarctic Fur Seal makes it easy to pick out among a mass of Antarctic Fur Seals.

1m

① Subantarctic Fur Seal
Arctocephalus tropicalis

DISTRIBUTION: Subantarctic islands and their beaches, especially Gough, Amsterdam and Marion Islands.

IDENTIFICATION: Similar in size and shape to the Antarctic Fur Seal (*page 114*), but bulls, the usual visitors to South Georgia, have a sandy 'bib' covering the face and chest that contrasts with dark brown upperparts. A small raised hairy crest is apparent on the forehead. Cows similar to Antarctic Fur Seals.

VOICE: Unmistakable in even a large colony of Antarctic Fur Seals, the higher-pitched 'woof' of this species is often the first indication that a visitor has arrived.

BEHAVIOUR: Similar to the Antarctic Fur Seal.

Rare visitor	
Length (male):	2·0 m
Length (female):	1·4 m
Weight (male):	100–160 kg
Weight (female):	35–50 kg

WHERE TO SEE: Among Antarctic Fur Seals.

① Southern Elephant Seal

Mirounga leonina

Resident	
SG:	400,000
GP:	740,000
Length (male):	4·0–5·0 m
Length (female):	2·6–3·0 m
Weight (male):	up to 4,500 kg
Weight (female):	800 kg

Threats: Protected but occasionally entangled in fishing gear.

WHERE TO SEE: On beaches around the island, rarely far from the water, or in muddy wallows behind the beaches during the moulting period. They are very rarely seen at sea, partly because they spend so little time at the surface.

DISTRIBUTION: The Southern Ocean. Breeding ranges from southern Argentina, Tristan da Cunha and Auckland Islands to the Antarctic mainland at 78°S. South Georgia is the main breeding stronghold.

IDENTIFICATION: Largest of all seals, the size and shape of bull elephant seals are unmistakable; look for the inflatable trunk-like nose which gives their name. Cows are much smaller and lack the distinctive nose but they are still huge compared to any other seal in the region except the largest Leopard Seals. Elephant seals of all ages are corpulent and lazy on land, except during the breeding season when bulls chase and fight competitors.

VOICE: Bellow at each other in annoyance or threat. Bulls use the inflatable nose as a trumpet in display. Humans approaching too close are greeted by explosive guttural sounds from the throat, together with an open-mouth display.

BEHAVIOUR: Elephant Seals come to land only to breed and moult. Adult bulls arrive on the breeding beaches in August and the pregnant cows come ashore in September and October and gather into harems of up to 100 animals dominated by the largest bulls ('beachmasters'). Bulls are fully-grown at 10–12 years. Most never breed and they rarely survive as beachmasters for more than two years. Black-coated pups are born a few days after their mothers' arrival at the colony. They are suckled for 23–25 days and grow from 44 kg to 180 kg. They are then abandoned but remain ashore for another 4–6 weeks as 'weaners' while they moult and learn to swim and feed.

The adults return to sea after breeding but come ashore again in summer to moult, gathering in muddy wallows. Unusually, the moult, which lasts 2–3 weeks, involves shedding not only the hair but also the skin to which it is attached.

Elephant seals are consummate divers and spend most of their time submerged. They can remain underwater for up to two hours and reach depths of 1,000 m. Their diet is mainly squid with some fish and crustaceans.

The size difference between bull and cow.

A bull is surrounded by his 'harem' of cows with their pups.

INSET: 'Weaners' abandoned by their mothers rest on the beach until it is time to go to sea.

Adult elephant seals gather in foul-smelling wallows while they moult into new coats.

1 Weddell Seal

Leptonychotes weddellii

DISTRIBUTION: Fast-ice region around Antarctica, occurring further south than any other wild mammal. A few small colonies on subantarctic islands.

IDENTIFICATION: Looking grey or brown from a distance, the dappled fur of Weddell Seals distinguishes them from all other seals at South Georgia. The long, often-curling, whiskers, relatively flat face, large eyes and apparent smile combine to give this seal a pleasing 'friendly' appearance.

VOICE: An extraordinary range of booms, chirps and whistles underwater but normally silent on land.

BEHAVIOUR: A docile species that often remains asleep or rolls on its side and raises a flipper when approached. Weddell Seals are solitary but gather in loose colonies to breed. Bulls hold territories underwater. Cows bear their pups in September on ice or, at South Georgia, ashore. Weaning is at about 45 days.

Resident	
SG:	<100
GP:	800,000
Length:	2·5–3·5 m
Weight:	400–600 kg
	Females are slightly larger

Threats: The small population at the very northern limit of its breeding range makes it vulnerable.

WHERE TO SEE: South Georgia has the most northerly breeding colony of Weddell Seals at Larsen Harbour and neighbouring coves. Little is known about this population. Seals can be seen there throughout the summer in low numbers. Sightings elsewhere around the island are unusual.

Weddell Seals find South Georgia a little too warm for their liking, so they often lie out on small patches of snow in summer. In the fast-ice zone, Weddell Seals use their teeth to keep breathing holes open in the ice, but at South Georgia there is no use for this habit.

The diet is mainly fish and cephalopods with some crustaceans.

1

A Weddell Seal with her full-grown pup.

⓵ Leopard Seal
Hydrurga leptonyx

Uncommon visitor, mainly in winter	
Length:	2·4–3·4 m
Weight:	200–590 kg
	Females are slightly larger

DISTRIBUTION: Circumpolar in the pack-ice zone but occurs on all subantarctic islands in smaller numbers, and vagrants sometimes swim to Australia or South America. Global population 220,000–440,000.

Threats: None.

WHERE TO SEE: Mostly a winter visitor to South Georgia. Occurs around the coast near concentrations of seals and penguins. Observations in summer are scarce. Often seen in the water but sometimes asleep on the beach.

IDENTIFICATION: Adults are larger than Weddell (*page 120*) or Crabeater Seals (*below*), although many of the Leopard Seals visiting South Georgia are smaller juveniles. Abnormally large head and mouth, spotted fur, and often a serpent-like shape. The name derives from the black spots on the fur particularly visible on the light-coloured throat. The pattern of these spots can be used for individual identification.

VOICE: Highly vocal underwater in the breeding season but normally silent out of water.

BEHAVIOUR: Breeding has never been recorded at South Georgia. Normally solitary. Haul out on ice floes and beaches, often deeply asleep. Often approach boats and people, usually out of curiosity but sometimes aggressively. Prey on penguins and seals, especially in spring and summer, and Leopard Seals are often seen lurking off colonies on the lookout for unwary prey. Penguins are brought to the surface and thrashed violently to tear off chunks of flesh. Fish and krill are more important in winter. The cusped, interlocking teeth, similar to those of the Crabeater Seal, are used for straining krill from the water.

⓶ Crabeater Seal
Lobodon carcinophagus

Rare visitor	
Length:	2·2–2·6 m
Weight:	200–300 kg

WHERE TO SEE: A rare visitor to South Georgia.

DISTRIBUTION: Crabeater Seals are normally found in the pack-ice zone around Antarctica. They are the most abundant seal in the world, numbering 15 million, and one of the most abundant of all wild mammals.

IDENTIFICATION: Smallest of the true seals on South Georgia. Distinguished from the Weddell Seal (*page 120*) by uniform colouration and more pointed face. The fur is silvery-grey to creamy white.

VOICE: Usually silent out of water.

BEHAVIOUR: Breeding has never been recorded at South Georgia. The name is misleading. Crabeater Seals consume krill, strained from the water by their specially-adapted, multi-cusped, interlocking teeth which form a sieve. They are most commonly seen lying on ice floes far south of South Georgia although they are known to range very widely at sea. For reasons as yet unknown, Crabeater Seals sometimes travel tens of kilometres inland, most famously in the Dry Valleys of Antarctica, where their bodies are preserved for millennia.

Many Crabeater Seals have deep linear scars on the body caused by attacks by Leopard Seals (when young) or Killer Whales.

CETACEANS

The two main groups of cetaceans are the baleen whales (Mysticeti) and toothed whales (Odontoceti).

The baleen whales have no teeth and gather food by sieving it from the water with two rows of baleen or whalebone plates suspended from the roof of the mouth. They possess two blowholes. The group includes the right whales, the Humpback Whale and the rorquals, which have short flippers compared with the Humpback.

The toothed whales have teeth instead of baleen. They possess a single blowhole. The group includes the sperm whales, beaked whales, dolphins and porpoises.

'Whale', 'dolphin' and 'porpoise' are not scientific terms. 'Whale' is usually used to describe a large cetacean. Smaller cetaceans are usually called dolphins (with beaks) or porpoises (without beaks). The Killer Whale is a large member of the dolphin family (Delphinidae). 'Porpoise' should refer only to the six species belonging to the family Phocoenidae.

FACING PAGE (TOP TO BOTTOM):
A huge Blue Whale blows explosively, showing its paired blowholes.

A Killer Whale attempts to drown a minke whale by preventing it from surfacing.

BELOW: A Humpback Whale breaching is one of the most exciting sights in the Southern Ocean.

Members of a large group of Killer Whales 'bowride' in front of a ship off the coast of South Georgia.

① Southern Right Whale
Eubalaena australis

Length:	12–17 m

Threats: Protected since 1937 but many were killed illegally between 1951 and 1971, in the SW Atlantic. They are now recovering from commercial exploitation. Currently there is a high, unexplained, calf mortality in Argentine waters.

DISTRIBUTION: Circumpolar distribution in the Southern Ocean. Animals around South Georgia have also been seen in a calving ground at Peninsula Valdes in Argentina. They are one of the commonest large whales in South Georgia waters.

IDENTIFICATION: A massive, very broad whale with black, sometimes slightly mottled grey, body. The large head is covered with yellowish or white raised callosities, which can be used for individual identification. The upper jaw is arched and narrow. There is no dorsal fin and the flukes are broad and pointed at the tip. Flippers resemble broad paddles.

Large V-shaped blow. (Humpbacks sometimes show a broadly similar blow.)

BEHAVIOUR: Often active at the surface, sometimes breaching and rolling. They can be curious about objects in the water and may allow ships to approach. Often show flukes when sounding. Found singly, in small groups (up to 10) or loose aggregations up to 100. There are recent reports of right whales in inshore waters, including Cumberland Bay.

② Humpback Whale
Megaptera novaeangliae

Length:	11–19 m

Threats: None.

DISTRIBUTION: A cosmopolitan species with a circumpolar distribution in the Southern Ocean. The most abundant large cetacean in nearshore waters around the Antarctic continent. Extended migrations to breeding and calving grounds in temperate/tropical waters. Humpbacks occurring at South Georgia breed mainly off Brazil. They are relatively very rare around South Georgia compared to the Antarctic Peninsula, because they were the earliest target when whaling began in South Georgia, seemingly wiping out any memory in the species of the rich feeding grounds. Slowly becoming more frequent in recent years.

IDENTIFICATION: Medium to large whale with broad back usually with a small, variable dorsal fin and conspicuous dorsal hump. The very long, broad pectoral flippers, white on the underside, are very distinctive. Raised nodules on the head. Large pigmented flukes distinctively scalloped on the trailing edge. The pattern on the underside of the flukes is unique to an individual and is used for recognition by researchers. Photographs can be submitted for cataloguing to http://199.33.141.23/alliedwhale/submit.htm

Varied, bushy, sometimes V-shaped, blow.

BEHAVIOUR: Generally found singly, in pairs or groups (up to 8). Can be very active at the surface: breaching, rolling and slapping the water with pectoral flippers and flukes. Curious, often spy-hopping or approaching ships, even touching stationary ships. Feeding may involve 'lunge-feeding': swimming vertically with its mouth open or 'bubble-netting':blowing a circle of bubbles to trap krill or fish.

① Antarctic Minke Whale
Balaenoptera bonaerensis

DATA DEFICIENT	
Length:	7–10 m

Threats: Subject to hunting around the Antarctic continent.

DISTRIBUTION: Circumpolar occasionally ranging north of the Antarctic convergence zone, often in coastal regions and also in association with pack ice.

IDENTIFICATION: The second smallest rorqual whale after the Common or Dwarf Minke Whale. A very pointed beak and a sickle-shaped dorsal fin in the middle of the back usually with a small dorsal fin. Coloration ranges from slate grey to dark brown (the latter if infested with diatoms), often with lighter chevrons on the flank. Surface with the beak slightly elevated.

Blow can be small and diffuse, or tall and thin.

BEHAVIOUR: Generally solitary or in small groups (up to 6), although larger aggregations are seen in feeding areas. Can be curious and active, spy-hopping, charging quickly at the surface and even bow-riding.

② Blue Whale
Balaenoptera musculus

ENDANGERED	
Length:	22–33 m

Threats: Hunted to less than 5% of the original southern hemisphere population, it is perhaps only now beginning to recover from commercial exploitation. Extraordinarily heavy exploitation around South Georgia in the 1920s.

DISTRIBUTION: Isolated populations around the Southern Ocean in offshore waters. Found near the ice-edge in summer and generally move north in winter months.

IDENTIFICATION: Massive, long animals with broad head and raised blowholes. Bodies mottled blue-grey, with a diminutive dorsal fin far back on the extremely long back. Flukes often shown when sounding. When below the surface they sometimes appear turquoise. Columnar and extremely tall (over 10 m) blow which appears significantly before the dorsal fin emerges.

BEHAVIOUR: Fast-swimming whales, generally solitary or in small groups (<5) or loose feeding aggregations. They are known to feed near the surface, sometimes rolling on their sides and lunging.

A very tall blow.

COMPARISON: The Common Minke Whale *Balaenoptera acutorostrata* probably occurs at South Georgia. The southern hemisphere form is called White-shouldered or Dwarf Minke Whale (*see page 132*) and is at least a separate subspecies from the northern hemisphere form. It is smaller than the antarctic species (maximum length less than 8 m) and is distinctively white on the upper face of the flipper which extends onto the shoulder.

① Sei Whale
Balaenoptera borealis

ENDANGERED	
Length:	14–20 m

Threats: None described. Recovering from commercial exploitation that ceased in the late 1960s.

DISTRIBUTION: Cosmopolitan, occasionally venturing to the ice-edge in summer months.

IDENTIFICATION: Large, sleek whale that is dark grey to blue-grey. There may be an orange tinge from a coating of diatoms in summer. A pointed snout and a large upright sickle-shaped dorsal fin. Surface with the dorsal fin exposed while breathing. Compared with the Fin Whale, the fin is more erect and has a straighter leading edge.

A moderately tall, vertical blow.

BEHAVIOUR: Generally solitary but sometimes seen in small groups (up to 8). Flukes are rarely shown when sounding. Typically less curious of ships. Feeding involves 'skimming' in which the whale swims through an aggregation of prey with its mouth open or 'swallowing' in which discrete gulps are taken.

② Fin Whale
Balaenoptera physalus

ENDANGERED	
Length:	17–25 m

Threats: None described. Recovering from heavy commercial exploitation.

DISTRIBUTION: Worldwide in temperate to polar waters, typically not venturing into the pack ice.

IDENTIFICATION: Sleek whales, dark grey to dark brown to bronze. May appear bronze during the summer when they have a coating of diatoms. There are lighter chevrons on the flanks below the blowholes. One of the few animals to have an asymmetrical coloration pattern: the lower right jaw is markedly white. The sloping dorsal fin is relatively conspicuous, and usually not exposed until after the head submerges, in contrast to the Sei Whale. The snout appears more pointed than the Blue Whale's. Tight, tall columnar blow.

BEHAVIOUR: They are fast swimming, may 'lunge-feed' near the surface by rolling on their sides, but rarely show flukes when sounding. Commonly seen in small groups large dispersed feeding groups (of up to 100) in South Georgia waters, often to the south and south-west of the island.

Species not recorded in South Georgia waters but their known range and habitat suggest that they may visit.

Pygmy Blue Whale
Balaenoptera musculus intermedia

Common Minke Whale
Balaenoptera acutorostrata

Gray's Beaked Whale
Cephalorhynchus eutropia

Hector's Beaked Whale
Cephalorhynchus hectori

Commerson's Dolphin
Cephalorhynchus commersonii

Peale's Dolphin
Lagenorhynchus australis

Southern Right Whale Dolphin
Lissodelphis peronii

COMPARISON: The Sei Whale is usually much smaller than the Fin Whale, though small (especially young) Fin Whales are smaller than the largest Sei Whales. Generally, as shown in the comparison above, the Sei Whale has a much more 'hooked' fin and will show a flatter profile from head to fin. Note the extent of back showing on the Fin Whale pictured below compared to the Sei Whale above. If seen well, a Fin Whale's white, right jaw (visible on both animals below) is diagnostic of the species.

COMPARISON:

Blue Whale: very large, blow taller and dorsal fin smaller and less curved than Fin Whale.

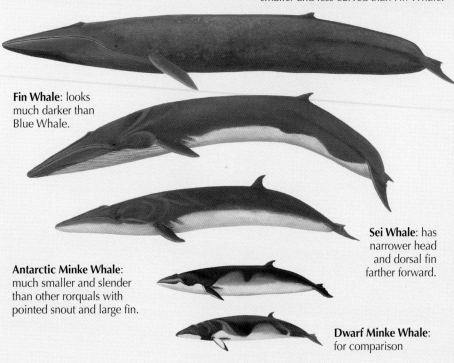

Fin Whale: looks much darker than Blue Whale.

Sei Whale: has narrower head and dorsal fin farther forward.

Antarctic Minke Whale: much smaller and slender than other rorquals with pointed snout and large fin.

Dwarf Minke Whale: for comparison

Humpback Whale: Dorsal hump, white flippers and white underside of the flukes.

Sperm Whale: Usually browner than Humpback Whale, with blowhole on the front of the head.

Southern Right Whale: No dorsal fin, large head covered with callosities.

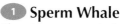 Sperm Whale

Physeter macrocephalus

DISTRIBUTION: Worldwide.

IDENTIFICATION: The largest toothed whale with a bulbous head that makes up one third of the body length and a narrow underslung lower jaw. Females are one third smaller but they do not enter the Southern Ocean. Often very wrinkled skin on the head unlike other species, thick triangular flukes and a low triangular dorsal ridge hump instead of a fin. Grey to black. There may be up to six protuberances on the back behind the fin.

Bushy blow canted forward from a single anterior blowhole at the front of the head, on lefthand side.

BEHAVIOUR: Adult males are solitary, in deep offshore waters. They are known to rest at the surface between deep dives and often show flukes when sounding. In South Georgia waters they interact with commercial long-line fishing by stealing Patagonian Toothfish from hooks.

VULNERABLE	
Length:	10–18 m

Threats: None described. Recovering from heavy commercial exploitation.

❶ Arnoux's Beaked Whale
Berardius arnuxii

Length: 7–10m

DISTRIBUTION: Southern hemisphere from temperate to polar waters and into loose pack ice. Generally in deep waters, but known to occur close to shore if the shelf is narrow.

IDENTIFICATION: Dark grey to dark brown, slender whale with well-defined melon and long beak, and a small, often triangular, dorsal fin. Two pairs of triangular teeth on the tip of the lower jaw of both sexes. Older animals of both sexes may have rake marks across their bodies caused from tooth-raking by conspecifics.

Low bushy blow.

BEHAVIOUR: Generally seen in small groups (6–12) but larger aggregations (up to 80) have been recorded. As deep divers they are rarely seen at the surface but have been observed in social groups, keeping close together and breathing in unison. Generally not curious of ships. The bulging melon and long beak are often shown when the whale surfaces.

❷ Southern Bottlenose Whale
Hyperoodon planifrons

Length: 6–9m

DISTRIBUTION: Circumpolar in southern hemisphere species from temperate to polar latitudes. Deep water generally offshore.

IDENTIFICATION: Generally more rotund than other beaked whales. Short beak and extremely bulbous melon often at an acute angle with the beak. Relatively tall dorsal fin far back. Dark grey to bronze. Adult males usually heavily scarred. Fin more pointed than Arnoux's Beaked Whale. A pair of teeth at the tip of the lower jaw erupt only in adult males.

Low, forward-canted, bushy blow.

BEHAVIOUR: Solitary or small groups, generally not at the surface very long. Surfaces with bulbous melon and beak showing simultaneously.

❸ Strap-toothed Beaked Whale
Mesoplodon layardii

DATA DEFICIENT

Length: 4–6m

DISTRIBUTION: Circumpolar below 30°S. Sometimes south of the polar front, in deep waters offshore.

IDENTIFICATION: Long white beak and small dorsal fin. Mostly blue-black to brown and a light grey-coloured back, with a black mask around the eyes and shoulders. Male has a pair of long tusks curving around upper jaw and the body is scarred.

BEHAVIOUR: Shy of boats. Found alone or in small groups up to 4. Often shows beak when surfacing.

Strap-toothed Beaked Whale

Southern Bottlenose Whale

Arnoux's Beaked Whale

1 **Killer Whale**

Orcinus orca

Length: 7–9 m

DISTRIBUTION: Cosmopolitan in offshore and coastal waters. Occasionally in oceanic waters.

IDENTIFICATION: The largest of the dolphin family, adult males have tall (1·5–2·0 m) dorsal fins, others have large sickle or triangular fins and a bulbous round head. Large paddle-like flippers. Strikingly distinctive black and white colour pattern with a conspicuous white patch behind the eye and white-grey saddle around the dorsal fin.

Tall, bushy blow.

Four 'ecotypes' of Killer Whale (**Types A**, **B**, **C** and **D**), based on appearance and diet, are recognised in antarctic waters and it has been suggested that they represent at least three separate species. **Types A**, **B** and **D** have been observed around South Georgia.

Type A is variable in size but usually large, and is black and white with a medium-sized, oval eye-patch roughly parallel to the body axis. In Antarctic waters it preys mainly on Antarctic Minke Whales.

Type B is similar but grey, black and white and has variable eye-patch that can be as much as twice the size of **Type A**'s. A dark grey dorsal cape, visible in good light, runs from the saddle to the eye-patch and contrasts with the paler flank; often appears yellowish from diatoms. It preys mainly on seals but also takes Antarctic Minke Whales. A smaller form of **Type B** that occurs in the Peninsula area, and possibly at South Georgia, preys upon penguins and possibly fish.

Type C is similar overall to **Type B** and has a distinct cape but it has a distinctively narrow, forward-slanting eye-patch. It preys on fish and has been recorded only in East Antarctica.

Type D is not well-known but it is easily recognised by the extremely small eye-patch, more bulbous head and more swept-back fin. It has been recorded in subantarctic seas and is believed to prey on fish.

BEHAVIOUR: Generally found in groups (5–20) which include one or more adult males and all other age/sex classes. Known to spy-hop (lift the head vertically out of the water to look around) and be active at the surface particularly when being social or hunting. Occasionally follow slow-moving ships. Steals Patagonian Toothfish from longlines.

Type A   Type B   Type C   Type D

1   **Type A**

1m   **Type B**

1f   **Type C**

1m   **Type D**

① Long-finned Pilot Whale
Globicephala melas

DATA DEFICIENT

Length: 4–7 m

DISTRIBUTION: Worldwide in mid to high latitudes, rarely as far south as ice edge.

IDENTIFICATION: Dorsal fin is extremely wide-based and falcate (females and young) or heavily lobed (adult males) set far forward. Head blunt, rounded. Black with small white eye-stripes extending up and back behind the eyes and often a white-grey saddle around the dorsal fin.

Small blow.

BEHAVIOUR: Found in moderate to large groups (10–100, but up to 500) including animals of all age/sex classes. Can be curious of passing ships often coalescing into linear groups at the surface. Regularly seen with other dolphin or whale species.

② Hourglass Dolphin
Lagenorhynchus cruciger

Length: 1·4–2·0 m

DISTRIBUTION: Mid to high latitudes, circumpolar in the Southern Ocean. Oceanic waters, fairly common in the Drake Passage and Scotia Sea.

IDENTIFICATION: Small dolphin. Small beak, black and white body with distinctive white hourglass-shaped markings on the length of the flanks. Female has sickle-shaped dorsal fin; male's is much more lobed.

BEHAVIOUR: Typically in small groups up to 12 but sometimes larger groups of 50–100. Often bow or stern-riding, porpoising or swimming quickly just below the surface.

③ Spectacled Porpoise
Phocoena dioptrica

DATA DEFICIENT

Length: 1·2–2·0 m

DISTRIBUTION: Circumpolar. Oceanic and coastal waters.

IDENTIFICATION: Dark grey-black dorsal surface contrasts with white undersides and flukes. White spectacle around a dark eye. Small almost completely white flippers. Distinctive large broad and round dorsal fin, especially of male. Black lips and small head.

BEHAVIOUR: Seen alone or in small groups up to 3–5.
Fast swimming below the surface with slow rolls at surface when breathing.

Spectacled Porpoise

Hourglass Dolphin

Long-finned Pilot Whale

Of the total of 14 species of mammal introduced to South Georgia (*page 19*) only three survived in the wild. Brown Rats and House Mice were introduced accidentally, with the former becoming a serious pest. Reindeer are the only deliberately-introduced mammals to survive . Rabbits survived for a few years before dying out.

Reindeer
Rangifer tarandus

Length:	Male	162–205 cm
	Female	180–214 cm

DISTRIBUTION: Between 1911 and 1925, whalers introduced 22 Reindeer from Norway. Their descendants now number around 3,000 animals. The herds occupy two discrete areas: Barff Peninsula (including St Andrews Bay and Royal Bay), and the majority of Busen Peninsula (including Stromness Bay and Fortuna Bay). The current range is limited by glaciers that prevent further spread.

IDENTIFICATION: A short-legged (80–150cm at shoulder), heavily built deer with tan to dark brown fur, fading to cream or white on throat and chest. Both males and females carry antlers. Antlers of males are massive and branched compared to simpler and more slender antlers of females.

Impact: South Georgia's relatively species-poor flora has evolved in the absence of herbivores and, as a consequence, copes poorly with grazing. Severe overgrazing of tussac and burnet communities has resulted in areas of erosion. Macrolichens have been locally eradicated. Reindeer are associated with the spread of the introduced Annual Meadow-grass which resists grazing far better than native species. Exclusion experiments have demonstrated that the native vegetation can recover in the absence of Reindeer (*see page 23*).

Brown, Common or Norway Rat
Rattus norvegicus

Length: Head and body   18–25 cm
 Tail   15–21 cm

Impact: Rats feed on eggs and chicks of ground-nesting birds and have had a significant impact on small burrowing seabirds, and to a lesser extent on the larger White-chinned Petrel and South Georgia Pintail. The South Georgia Pipit is almost entirely excluded from areas occupied by rats. Rats also feed on insects, seeds, Tussock Grass roots, marine invertebrates and carrion.

DISTRIBUTION: Rats were introduced accidentally from around 1800 by sealers and later by whalers. Their inability to cross glaciers has limited their range largely to the northwest of the island and northeast coast, especially in dense coastal tussac and around abandoned whaling stations. They range up to 3 km inland. At present rats occupy approximately one fifth of the island's total area and significantly more of the snow-free area. They are mostly absent from islands.

IDENTIFICATION: A large, stocky rodent with a rounded muzzle which may be seen out in daylight. The thick tail is shorter than the head and body length and has a pale underside. Coarse shaggy fur, dark brown on back, grey brown on flanks and pale grey on belly and throat. Juveniles are sleeker with finer, greyer fur.

SIGNS: Droppings: 13–19 mm long.
Footprints and 'runs': clearly defined and obvious in sand, mud and snow.
Burrow: 40–70mm wide.

House Mouse
Mus domesticus

Length: Head and body   6–9 cm
 Tail   7–10 cm

Impact: Unknown.

DISTRIBUTION: The full range on South Georgia is not known. Mice have been found on the rat-free Nuñez Peninsula up to Cape Rosa. They are likely to be more widely spread, as suggested by recent sightings. House Mice live in tussac bogs. They feed on seeds, insects, roots and carrion. They have adapted well to conditions on the island, as shown by a body size above average for the species.

IDENTIFICATION: A small, slender rodent with a long thin tail the same length or longer than the head and body length. The short fine fur is grey/brown, with grey or white belly. Dark, nearly black, colour forms have been seen on South Georgia.

SIGNS: Droppings: 4–7 mm long, found in large numbers in small clusters.
Burrow: 22–47 mm wide.

There are almost 200 species of invertebrates known to live on South Georgia which, by world standards, is a very small number for an island of this size. This number is likely to increase as most are in groups of unfamiliar small animals and many have not been studied by appropriate specialists on South Georgia. The numbers of species are limited by the island's isolation and extreme weather. Invertebrates can survive only if they are highly resistant to freezing when overwintering or if they colonise human habitation.

Most of South Georgia's invertebrates are tiny and inconspicuous, and only a small number are easily identified in the field. Apart from a number of endemic species the native invertebrate fauna is largely derived from the southern mountains and bogs of the Andes, Tierra del Fuego and the Falkland Islands, and many also live on other subantarctic islands. Alien species from various parts of the world have colonised the island, some with deleterious effects on the native species.

Hydromedion sparsutum

Perimylops antarcticus

INSECTS

Beetles: Coleoptera

Tussac beetles:

GR:	South Georgia (endemic)

The two plant/detritus-eating tussac beetles are the largest and most conspicuous ground-dwelling insects. The more common tussac beetle *Hydromedion sparsutum* (8 mm long) is common everywhere where there is longer vegetation or damp debris to crawl under. It is also often found walking over late-lying snow. It is variable in colour from plain black, through bronze, dark brown almost to orange and usually has brown or orange legs. It is in some decline as a result of predation by the introduced

Hydromedion sparsutum larva

Perimylops antarcticus larva

ground beetles. The second species *Perimylops antarcticus* (6–8 mm long) is plain black with thinner, black legs and is found only among very sparse vegetation, on high fellfields and stony river margins. The grubs of both species are difficult to tell apart and are long, thin and segmented, with a pair of erect 'spikes' at their rear end.

Ground beetles
Trechisibus antarcticus and
Merizodus soledadinus   (4–5 mm long)

GR:	South America, Falkland Islands

Alien invasives that both come from South America/the Falklands and spreading from Husvik and/or Grytviken where they arrived around 30 years ago. The two species are difficult reliably to tell apart. Both are shiny bronze-black and fast running. Unfussy about where they

Trechisibus antarcticus

Merizodus soledadinus

live, both can be found under loose stones and debris, in moss, tussac and other plant litter. They are general predators on other invertebrates and have damaging effects on populations of other species, especially tussac beetles and perhaps rove beetles and the flightless midge.

Lancetes angusticollis

Water beetle
Lancetes angusticollis   (8 mm long)

GR:	Southern South America

A diving beetle that is easily identified because it is the only large invertebrate found in fresh water, where it can most easily be seen coming to the surface, often among submerged moss, to breathe through its rear end. Its larva looks quite different, being long and thin with huge jaws. It inhabits almost any freshwater body on South Georgia: lakes and tarns, the less violent streams and rivers and even old elephant seal wallows.

Lancetes angusticollis larva

Rove beetle
Halmaeusa atriceps   (3·5 mm long)

GR:	Subantarctic islands

The only elongate red and black beetle currently is common in a wide variety of habitats, from tussac litter, moss, under stones especially by streams, to seaweed in the strandline on the beach. It is possibly predatory or it may eat fungi on plant litter. Recent studies suggest it might be in decline where alien ground beetles occur.

Halmaeusa atriceps

Pill beetle
Chalicosphaerium sp.   (4·5 mm long)

A small globular metallic beetle, either emerald green or brown/bronze.
A breeding colony of this little pill beetle was first found on South Georgia at Grytviken in 2009 where it was abundant in small areas of deep moss (which it probably eats) with fescue grass. It is new to science and not yet named, but all related species live in South America and the Falkland Islands.

Chalicosphaerium sp.

Flies: Diptera

Flightless non-biting midge
Eretmoptera murphyi   (3 mm long)

GR:	South Georgia (endemic), introduced to South Orkney Islands

A small grey fly with very tiny wing remnants is endemic to South Georgia. It is occasionally found scuttling about among tussac litter and short grass, including the introduced Annual Meadow Grass. It breeds in wet peaty soil. It is the one endemic South Georgian species that has been accidentally introduced elsewhere: to Signy Island in the South

Eretmoptera murphyi

Orkney Islands where it is spreading. This species is vulnerable to predation by the introduced ground beetles and appears now not to live where they occur.

Non-biting midge
Parochlus steinenii (2 mm long)

GR:	Andean South America, Tierra del Fuego, subantarctic islands, maritime antarctic islands

One of the most abundant flying insects with a black body and clear wings. It is usually found quite near the streams, lakes or saturated moss in which it breeds. Often there are mass emergences of tens of thousands, either flying over water or forming living carpets on, or even under, rocks.

Winter gnat
Trichocera regelationis (6 mm long)

GR:	Europe, northern Asia, North America, introduced to Falkland Islands

This fly has a narrow body with legs to 10mm and with brown spotted wings. Winter gnats are often mistaken for mosquitos. They live in tussac and fly around the litter 'skirts' of tussocks. It was almost introduced by whalers who brought Norwegian soil to place on graves.

Kelp fly
Antrops truncipennis (4 mm long)

GR:	South Georgia (endemic)

This flightless insect is grey-brown with orange-red eyes and a quite flattened body. It lives only among dead kelp and other dead seaweed on the beach and rapidly scuttles down between stones when disturbed. It only lives on South Georgia. There are also a couple of similar-looking, but winged, species found in the same situations which are more widespread on subantarctic islands.

Parochlus steinenii

Trichocera regelationis

Antrops truncipennis

Eristalis croceimaculata

Calliphora vicina

Hover fly
Eristalis croceimaculata   (12 mm long)

GR:	Southern South America, Falkland Islands

Hairy, dark brown and orange with clear wings, most likely to be seen on Dandelion and buttercup flowers around Grytviken. A recent colonist to South Georgia, this species was only caught and identified in 2009. Given its discovery at Grytviken and Stromness, it is likely to have arrived on visiting ships. Its larvae have yet to be found on South Georgia but they are likely to live in peaty water or very wet mud, or possibly in seal wallows. Its presence on the island may help the spread of alien invasive, insect-pollinated plants such as Cow Parsley and Creeping Buttercup.

Flesh fly or Bluebottle
Calliphora vicina   (8–10 mm long)

GR:	Probably originally European but now worldwide

A typical bluebottle fly with a dusty blue body, dull red eyes and clear wings, often visiting flowers or basking in sunshine on stones. A recent colonist and flower visitor, this species was originally found in the Grytviken area and has spread rapidly east and west, at least as far as Fortuna Bay and Moltke Harbour in 2009. Its maggot lives in dead animals – seals, Reindeer and birds and it may compete with native flies. Like the hoverfly, it may help the spread of alien invasive plants.

SPRINGTAILS: Collembola

Formerly included with the insects, these are one of several groups of flightless arthropods that have now been placed in their own group that is primitive to the true insects. Perhaps the most distinctive is *Sminthurinus jonesi*. This tiny (less than 1 mm) fat springtail is variable in colour from black, to grey brown or parti-coloured. It lives only in South Georgia and is named after its discoverer, Neville Jones, of the British Antarctic Survey, in the 1960s. Other springtails (of which there are around 20 species) on South Georgia are much slimmer. They are often very abundant under stones, in moss, litter and fungi. Several non-native species are also established, with one, *Hypogastrura viatica*, being quite widespread.

Sminthurinus jonesi

A mass of springtails floating on the surface of a puddle.

Notiomaso flavus

Notiomaso sp. egg sacs

ARACHNIDS

Spiders: Aranaeae

GR:	Some species are endemic, others also inhabit South America and Falkland Islands

There are five money spiders on South Georgia which are very difficult to tell apart, all being shining blackish brown, 2 to 5mm long. One species, *Notiomaso grytvikensis* named after the whaling station, has subsequently been found in the Falkland Islands. They occur under stones, in moss, in tussac litter - anywhere there is cover. Their silken egg sacs are common under stones.

Mites and Ticks: Acari

There are more than 70 species of mites on South Georgia. Their maximum size is less than 2mm but they form the most diverse group of animals on the island

Ixodes kerguelensis

and are extremely abundant in some habitats. A very specialist knowledge is needed to tell them apart. There are species of the seashore, plant litter and moss beds, while some species occur in tiny cracks in rocks at high altitude. Others live among the feathers of birds.

Antarctic Bird Tick
Ixodes kerguelensis (2·5 mm long)

GR:	Pacific islands, south Australia, subantarctic islands

Very flat and slow-moving, lives among the feathers of seabirds and sucks their blood. It is sometimes found on the ground where there are seabirds, especially on the beach and in old nests. It does not bite people!

FRESHWATER CRUSTACEANS

There are many species of planktonic animals in lakes and tarns on South Georgia. Most are very tiny (much less than 1mm long). Some are bright red.

Copepod water flea
Parabroteas sarsi (9·5 mm long)

GR:	Andean South America and sub- and maritime antarctic freshwaters

At nearly 1cm long, this is the largest free-living copepod in the world. It carries its eggs in a sac under its tail.

Parabroteas sarsi

ANNELIDS

Earthworms: Oligochaeta

There are three species of earthworm on South Georgia. Two small yellow worms, *Microscolex georgianus* and *crosstenis* (up to 3cm long), live mainly in wet tussac litter and occur also in southern South America and the Falklands. *Dendrodrilus rubidus* is a larger pink species (up to 8cm long) and is an alien originally from Europe but now cosmopolitan. It is common everywhere on South Georgia, often under stones, in moss and even in shallow water.

Microscolex georgianus

Dendrodrilus rubidus

MOLLUSCS

Snails: Gastropoda

Land snail
Notodiscus hookeri

A small population of a tiny land snail (adult shells 2·5 to 3·5 mm diameter) was discovered in 1970 about 1 km north of King Edward Point. The snails occur near the base of a high cliff near the shore on mosses, in crevices and pockets of soil on ledges. They appear to feed on lichens, algae or cyanobacteria. It is thought that the species was brought to South Georgia from islands in the southern Indian Ocean by seabirds.

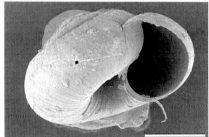

Notodiscus hookeri

PLANTS

'**Higher plants**' consist of the flowering and seed-producing plants and the spore-producing ferns and fern-like plants. They are grouped together because they have evolutionarily advanced structures, notably specialised tissues for conducting, throughout the plant's body, water, nutrients from the soil and carbohydrates manufactured by photosynthesis.

Herbs are non-woody flowering plants that are divided into 'grass-like' (graminoids) and 'non-grasslike' (forbs).

'**Lower plants**' consist of the mosses, liverworts and algae which lack these specialised structures.

Higher plants

South Georgia's native higher plant flora comprises only 25 species including one hybrid. All are perennial and herbaceous (i.e. not woody).

About another 60 species of alien plants have been recorded and currently about 35–40 have become naturalised, i.e. have survived for more than 50 years on the island. A few are represented by only a small number of long-lived individual plants. Most of these introductions occurred in and around the whaling stations as a result of seeds imported unintentionally in cargo and building materials brought from northern Europe. More significantly, seeds were imported with fodder for sheep, poultry and other domestic animals. Only the most widespread and prominent species are described in the following pages.

Some naturalised plants have spread and a few have displaced native species. Many of these plants only grew in sheltered conditions in the whaling stations and died out shortly after the end of the whaling era (mid-1960s). In the early 2000s a major clean-up of the Grytviken station and buildings has resulted in the rapid spread of many of the naturalised aliens, the reappearance of some supposedly extinct species from seed that had survived in the soil, and the establishment of many new species. Ground disturbance and use of vehicles, together with increasingly warm summers which allow plants to set viable seed, have greatly aided their spread. The recent appearance of flies that can transfer pollen may also encourage seed setting and increased dispersal.

Throughout the 20th century a number of plants were grown for food or ornament, such as tomatoes and daffodils, in greenhouses, conservatories and on window ledges in the whaling stations and the community at King Edward Point. None became naturalised and the growing of alien plants is now banned (*see page 22*).

LEFT: Antarctic Pearlwort; RIGHT: Greater Burnet

Tussock Grass with a carpet of
Antarctic Pearlwort;

BELOW: Brown Rush

Greater Burnet
Acaena magellanica

Native

GR: Patagonia, Falkland Islands, subantarctic islands

A low (5–20 cm) shrub-like herb with intertwining woody stems. The leaves comprise 4–6 pairs of dark to bluish-green leaflets, somewhat rounded at the apex, with slightly serrated margins. In early summer these usually have a reddish tinge. The prominent globular (1–2 cm diameter) inflorescences (*inset*) are borne on the end of a 5–15 cm long stem; these comprise a cluster of tiny inconspicuous florets each producing a seed with 4 spines each tipped with a barb. When ripe in late summer these attach very readily to clothing, fur seal fur and bird feathers and are very difficult to remove. Leaves are edible with a bitter taste and were eaten by early sealers and whalers to stave off scurvy.

WHERE TO SEE: Widespread and abundant among most vegetation types and often forming large swathes on sheltered moist slopes.

ALTITUDE: 1–300 m.

Lesser Burnet
Acaena tenera

Native

GR: Patagonia, Falkland Islands, subantarctic islands

Resembling Greater Burnet but it is more prostrate and smaller in all its parts. The leaves also comprise 4–6 leaflets but are a dark, distinctly glossy green with a reddish toothed margin. The globular (3–7 mm diameter) inflorescence tops a 3–8 cm stem, and each seed bears 4 barbed spines that readily attach to clothing.

WHERE TO SEE: Widespread among most vegetation types, but more frequent in drier, stonier windswept habitats.

ALTITUDE: 1–>600 m.

❸ Hybrid Burnet
Acaena magellanica × tenera

Native (endemic)

GR: South Georgia

This is a cross between Greater and Lesser Burnets and is the only hybrid in the genus *Acaena*. In most respects its appearance is closer to Greater Burnet although the leaves are generally smaller and have a stronger bluish tinge. The best distinguishing feature is that the flowering stem bears a secondary, smaller, flower cluster on a very short stem in the axil of a small leaf about half way along the main flowering stem.

WHERE TO SEE: Widespread, but typically forming a narrow zone at the edge of stands of Greater Burnet. Mainly at lower altitudes.

ALTITUDE: 1–300 m.

Blinks
Montia fontana

Native

GR: Bipolar in cool temperate regions

A prostrate to loosely erect plant with straggling shoots 2–5 (10) cm long. The slightly succulent, reddish-purple (in spring) to yellow-green leaves are arranged in pairs along the stem, and are distinctly spoon-shaped, 5–10 mm long, with a pinkish central vein. Like Antarctic Bedstraw it has small white flowers (*inset*), but with only two sepals, three stamens and five round-tipped petals. One of only three species with distinctive petals (see also Antarctic Bedstraw (*below*) and Antarctic Buttercup (*page 158*)).

WHERE TO SEE: Fairly common, mainly on the mid central north side of the island, but easily overlooked when not flowering and may resemble Antarctic Starwort. Occurs mainly in damp habitats, usually among mosses in seepage areas, stream and pool margins, and on rock ledges.

ALTITUDE: near sea level to 160 m.

2 Antarctic Starwort
Callitriche antarctica

Native

GR: Patagonia, Falkland Islands, subantarctic islands

A compact, prostrate or shortly erect, bright green plant, with 5–10 cm long shoots, forming small mats on muddy surfaces. It also grows in water where the shoots become long (30–45 cm), loose and straggling. The oblong rounded leaves (2–5 mm) are in pairs along the stem. The flowers are only conspicuous when the anthers of the male flowers are mature, appearing as cream-white blobs among the leaves. There are no petals, but the sugar-producing nectaries attract small insects for pollination.

WHERE TO SEE: Widespread in coastal areas, especially around the base of Tussock Grass, around seal wallows, and stream and pond margins where it may form a floating mat extending up to 1 m from the water's edge.

ALTITUDE: 1–30 (75) m.

3 Antarctic Bedstraw
Galium antarcticum

Native

GR: Patagonia, Falkland Islands, subantarctic islands

A small, slender trailing plant, usually with sparse shoots up to 10 cm long, although occasionally quite dense and compact. The narrow, elliptical, dark green leaves (3–6 mm long) are arranged in whorls of four along the stem. The small 3- or 4-petalled flowers (*inset*) are white with a faint vanilla scent. Petals slightly triangular. One of only three species with distinctive petals (see also Antarctic Buttercup (*page 158*) and Blinks (*above*)).

WHERE TO SEE: Fairly common, mainly on the central north side of the island, especially in dry fescue grassland, on rock ledges and at the foot of rock faces.

ALTITUDE: sea level to 250 m.

❶ Antarctic Pearlwort
Colobanthus quitensis

This plant is often recognised by its compact dome-shaped cushion composed of a mass of radiating rosettes, each comprising a cluster of narrow, sharp-pointed, yellow-green leaves (5–7 mm). The cushions reach about 3–5 cm tall and 5–10 (20) cm across, but these often coalesce to form larger cushions or mats. The small yellowish flowers (*inset*) are formed by the sepals (there are no petals) and the prominent anthers are borne on short stalks <1 cm long.

Native

GR: Patagonia, Falkland Islands, subantarctic islands, Antarctica

WHERE TO SEE: Common in moist, well-drained coastal areas but extending into drier, stonier areas inland and to the most extreme habitats on the island.

ALTITUDE: 1–300 (500) m.

❷ Sessile or Subantarctic Pearlwort
Colobanthus subulatus

Very similar to Antarctic Pearlwort but forming larger, tightly compact, hard, emerald green cushions up to 20 cm high and 5–20 (60) cm across. The tight rosettes are composed of short, rigid, narrow, sharp-pointed leaves. The anthers protruding from the small, almost closed, buds of the inconspicuous flowers, without petals, are almost embedded in the leaf rosettes.

Native

GR: Patagonia, Falkland Islands, subantarctic islands

WHERE TO SEE: Common, but restricted to rocky areas close to the shore.

ALTITUDE: near sea level to over 100 m where its habitat is influenced by drifting sea spray.

❸ Mouse-ear Chickweed
Cerastium fontanum

With the exception of Annual Meadow Grass (*page 164*), this is the most widely distributed alien plant on the island. Each plant comprises numerous radiating shoots, 5–15 cm long. The leaves are ovoid, 5–10 mm long, and covered with whitish downy hairs giving a woolly appearance. Flowering stems, 7–15 cm long, bear loose clusters of flowers (*inset*), each approx. 2–3 mm diameter, with five white petals with a terminal notch.

Introduced

GR: Worldwide

WHERE TO SEE: Frequent on dry gravelly ground, moraines, outwash debris and river shingle but also among various native communities. Widely distributed in Reindeer areas and common in whaling stations.

ALTITUDE: 1–300 m.

Antarctic Buttercup
Ranunculus biternatus

A prostrate, far-creeping, to short erect plant with mid- to dark green, slightly fleshy leaves. These comprise three or more deeply divided leaflets, 1·0–2·5 cm across, each subdivided into three-pointed lobes, and with a stem of up to 5 cm long. The bright yellow flowers (7–10 mm diameter) near ground level have five (occasionally four) round-tipped petals and numerous stamens (*inset*). In late summer it produces a red to purple raspberry-like fruit. The acrid leaves are edible and were used as an antiscorbutic by sealers; the berry is also edible but bitter.

Native

GR: Patagonia, Falkland Islands, subantarctic islands

WHERE TO SEE: Common in damp to wet habitats amongst bogs and mires, seepage areas, stream and pool margins, wet rock ledges, and occasionally drier fescue and open tussac grassland, also whaling stations.

ALTITUDE: 0–250 (300) m.

Creeping Buttercup
Ranunculus repens

A prominent flowering alien but much less common than Dandelion. The flower has five golden-yellow, rounded petals on stems 3–10 cm long. The leaves are deeply and sharply lobed, approx. 3–8 cm across and 5–15 cm tall. The spreading shoots produce patches up to 1 m diameter.

Introduced

GR: Eurasia
Americas, New Zealand (introduced)

WHERE TO SEE: Several spreading patches up to approx. 1 m across occur within Grytviken whaling station and also near the track at the east end of King Edward Point and at other whaling stations.

ALTITUDE: 2–15 m.

Dandelion
Taraxacum officinale

Probably the most conspicuous flower on the island, providing a brilliant display of yellow composite flowers. Each flower head, 2–4 cm diameter and comprising a dense mass of narrow elongated petals, is borne on a hollow fleshy stalk 5–20 cm long. As the seeds develop, each has a fine stalk topped by a cluster of hairs, the whole seed head forming a fluffy sphere. The clumps of bright green leaves (10–20 cm by 1–3 cm), have a distinct central vein and an undulating, broadly toothed margin. One route for its introduction was as seeds in soil from Norway that was placed on whalers' graves.

Introduced

GR: Northern hemisphere

WHERE TO SEE: Although present at all stations, recent vehicular activity in and around Grytviken has been responsible for a rapid and extensive spread of this species, particularly at King Edward Point and the hillside above the south side of King Edward Cove. Elsewhere, Reindeer have aided its spread. Its young leaves and flowers are a pleasant addition to a salad.

ALTITUDE: 1–65 m.

Bittercress
Cardamine glacialis*

This small plant has clusters of four-petalled flowers, 1–2 mm across, on short stems 1–3 cm long. The dark green leaves, 1–4 cm long, comprise a number of oval leaflets arranged along the leaf stem. A long, 1–3 cm, seed pod releases seeds explosively when ripe. Ranging from scattered individuals to large and dense aggregations of plants.

Introduced

GR: South America

WHERE TO SEE: First appearing on King Edward Point in 2002 and it has spread very rapidly and extensively over the Point and, since 2008, has appeared on the south side of King Edward Cove and in Grytviken. Several attempts to eradicate it have failed and it now poses a serious threat as it progressively invades the natural vegetation.

ALTITUDE: 1–10 m.

 Yarrow or **Milfoil**
Achillea millefolium

This perennial herb has a creeping woody stem forming a mat of interwoven plants. The distinctive finely-divided, feathery basal leaves (5–15 cm long) form a prostrate mass. Flowering stems up to 10–15 cm high have much shorter leaves and a terminal flat-topped cluster (2–4 cm across) of fragrant, white 5-petalled flowers, each 3–5 mm diameter and 3-toothed at the apex.

Introduced

GR: Eurasia, North America, Australia, New Zealand (introduced)

WHERE TO SEE: Known only as a large patch several metres across by the stream in front of the church in Grytviken, where it has persisted for over 50 years.

ALTITUDE: 5 m.

 Sheep's Sorrel
Rumex acetosella

This species forms small populations recognised from a distance by its reddish colour. Individual plants have reddish-margined, green, elongated round-tipped leaves, about 5–10 cm by 0·5–1·0 cm. The flowers consist of a loose aggregation of tiny reddish florets borne along a red, angled stem up to 20 cm long. Its leaves are edible but bitter.

Introduced

GR: Europe

WHERE TO SEE: Most frequent in and behind Grytviken and on a raised beach at Husvik.

ALTITUDE: 1–25 m.

*See taxonomic notes *page 188*.

Tussock Grass
Poa flabellata

A very large, robust plant arising from pedestals up to 1 m diameter formed by decaying leaves and roots that may be many decades or even centuries old in plants 1–2 m tall. The long leaves (30–100 cm) are broad (10–20 mm wide) and bright to dark green, but yellow-green in drier habitats. They are slightly keeled (V-shaped) in section and have a distinct groove running the length of the upper surface. The flowering stem (30–100 cm) bears a terminal compact, soft tufted inflorescence 5–12 cm long (*inset*). The evergreen leaves and carbohydrate-rich bases of the stems have sustained Reindeer and rats. The nutty-flavoured shoot bases were eaten by sealers and whalers, and are a tasty addition to a salad.

'Tussock' and 'tussac' are alternative spellings. In this book 'Tussock Grass' refers to the plant and 'tussac' to the community (*page 25*).

Native
GR: Patagonia, Falkland Islands, Gough Island

WHERE TO SEE: Widespread and very common around all coastal areas, forming a zone of dense tussac grassland behind most beaches. 'Tussac' is the name usually given to this type of grassland in the Falkland Islands. As the grass penetrates inland it becomes more scattered and its colour changes from dark green (nutrient-enriched habitats) to yellowish-green (drier, nutrient-poor habitats).

ALTITUDE: 0– approx. 150 m (to 300 m in major seabird habitats).

Brown or **Tufted Fescue**
Festuca contracta

An erect densely tufted grass. The long rigid leaves, 10–20 (–30) cm long, are strongly channelled and usually rolled to form a cylinder in cross section, and are dark- to bluish-green, but tinged purple in early summer. The old brown leaves remain on the plant for several years, giving it a dead appearance. The flower stalks (10–25 cm) bear a compact, finely-pointed terminal inflorescence, distinctly purple-coloured in spring.

Native
GR: Patagonia, Falkland Islands, subantarctic islands

WHERE TO SEE: Widespread, dominating large swathes of dry hillside and forming distinctive light brown grassland, particularly on the mid-north coast, but also scattered among most other plant communities.

ALTITUDE: 0–250 (400) m.

Red Fescue
Festuca rubra

This erect darkish green, tall (15–30 cm) grass forms quite large stands. The leaves are usually rolled into a cylinder, but may be flat (1–2 mm wide) with a coarse upper surface. The flowering spikes are usually taller than the leaves and the inflorescences – at first appressed tightly to the stem; become feathery later and have a reddish tinge.

Introduced
GR: Eurasia, North Africa, North America

WHERE TO SEE: Particularly common within Grytviken and King Edward Point.

ALTITUDE: 2–10 m.

1 Alpine Cat's-tail
Phleum alpinum

This grass occurs in two forms. In dry stony habitats plants are prostrate with short spreading leaves (5–10 cm by 3–8 mm) and few flower stems (5–10 cm); in moist sheltered habitats plants are erect (leaves to 8–20 cm) and have large numbers of short, cylindrical inflorescences (2–4 cm) borne on 15–35 cm long stems. It resembles Magellanic Foxtail but has broader pale green leaves tinged purple in early summer.

Native

GR: Patagonia, bipolar

WHERE TO SEE: Widespread and common in most plant communities, especially dry gravelly habitats, mainly on the mid-northern coast; elsewhere scarce.

ALTITUDE: 0–>375 m.

2 Magellanic or Antarctic Foxtail
Alopecurus magellanicus

An erect grass with distinctive long, narrow, flattened blue-green leaves, 15–20 (–30) cm long and 3–4 mm broad. Each soft, silky, cylindrical, terminal inflorescence (2–4 cm long) is borne terminally on a flower stalk 15–50 cm long. May be confused with tall forms of Alpine Cat's-tail, but in that species the leaves are usually tinged purple, as are the somewhat spiky, coarser inflorescences.

Native

GR: Patagonia, Falkland Islands

WHERE TO SEE: Confined to the Stromness Bay area, especially from Olsen Valley to Shackleton Valley, and a single locality at Shallop Cove on the south coast. A small but increasing population also occurs at King Edward Point where it was introduced from Husvik in 1981. Locally abundant on dry gravel outwash areas, mires, at the margins of streams and pools, and occasionally amongst dry tussac grassland.

❶ Annual Meadow-grass
Poa annua

This short (2–7 cm), tufted, bright green grass prefers disturbed ground. Dislodged fragments readily become rooted, often resulting in extensive swards of closed grassland. The slightly keeled leaves are 1–2 mm broad with two parallel central veins running their full length; they often have transverse undulations towards the apex. Flowering shoots (*inset*) are fairly short, 5–10 (–15) cm, and the inflorescence is feathery. In early summer the leaves and flowers are tinged purple. On South Georgia the species exists as a perennial.

Introduced

GR: Worldwide

WHERE TO SEE: The most widespread invasive species, it occurs all around the island. It was probably introduced in the early 1800s by sealing expeditions. Locally very abundant on low ground, forming extensive 'lawns' especially in areas trampled by fur seals and grazed by Reindeer.

ALTITUDE: Scattered plants occur to 500 m.

❷ Smooth-stalked Meadow-grass
Poa pratensis

Frequently grows with the very similar Annual Meadow Grass but the leaves are usually much taller (7–25 cm) and with flowering stems 15–35 cm long.

Introduced

GR: Eurasia, North Africa, North America

WHERE TO SEE: Much more restricted to the vicinity of the whaling stations than Annual Meadow-grass, usually in damp areas.

ALTITUDE: Seldom occurs above approx. 75 m altitude.

❸ Common Bent-grass
Agrostis capillaris

This pale rusty brown grass, 15–30 cm tall, usually forms circular patches, up to several metres across. The leaves are narrow (1–2 mm wide) and taper to a fine point. The flower spikes terminate in a feathery inflorescence.

Introduced

GR: Eurasia, North America

WHERE TO SEE: On hillsides close to and within whaling stations.

ALTITUDE: Mainly from approx. 2–30 m.

1 Antarctic Hair-grass
Deschampsia antarctica

Native
GR: Patagonia, Falkland Islands, subantarctic islands, Antarctica

A green to yellowish-green grass of variable stature ranging from compact prostrate mats to erect clumps.
The narrow leaves, 3–10 (15) cm long and 1–2 mm wide are flattened and slightly furrowed on the upper surface. Each flowering shoot (5–20 cm) bears a finely branched, somewhat feathery inflorescence.

WHERE TO SEE: Widespread and often abundant, occurring in most habitats and among most plant communities. It forms extensive swards in damp coastal areas, especially where influenced by seals and penguins. Here, the grass develops a prostrate growth-form due largely to the effects of trampling, but in drier and more wind-exposed habitats, individual plants tend not to coalesce and are small and yellowish. In wet habitats unaffected by wildlife, plants may be tall, erect and darker green (*inset*).

ALTITUDE: 0–>500 m.

2 Tufted Hair-grass
Deschampsia cespitosa

Introduced
GR: Eurasia, North Africa, North America

This is the largest of the alien grasses. It forms circular patches 50–150 cm across. Leaves are long (25–50 cm by 1–3 mm), roughly grooved, with a finely serrated margin. The flower spikes are up to 50 cm long and the feathery terminal inflorescence is up to 10 cm long, with all spikelets curving to one side.

WHERE TO SEE: Frequent in and around Grytviken, less so at other whaling stations.

ALTITUDE: 2–60 m.

3 Smith's Sedge
Uncinia macrolepis

Native
GR: Andes Mountains of Colombia and Venezuela to Patagonia, Falkland Islands

This grass-like species spreads through the soil by a creeping rhizome from which arise clusters of leafy shoots. It is distinguished by the distinctly triangular cross-section of the stems. The light green to brownish-green leaves (8–15 cm long by 2–5 mm wide) are curved backwards, arranged in three rows along the stem and are V-shaped in section. The flowering stems (3–8 cm) bear a terminal flower spike which comprises a short cylindrical cluster of flowers (*inset*). Each seed bears a prominent hooked awn.

WHERE TO SEE: Widespread but scattered, especially in dry fescue grassland and occasionally in drier parts of mires, mainly on the mid-north coast.

ALTITUDE: 5–250 (375) m.

1 Greater Rush
Juncus scheuchzerioides

Grows as a loose, erect tufted mass of cylindrical pointed leaves, 3–12 (25) cm long, filled with a white pith and jointed at intervals along the blade. The leaves arise from an underground trailing rhizome, and are dark green, but distinctly reddish or purple in early summer especially after snow melt. The 2–3 small feathery flowers (*inset*) are borne on 1–3 cm long stems and later develop small orange-brown seed capsules, triangular in section. It is usually sterile in the wettest habitats.

Native

GR: Patagonia, Falkland Islands, Macquarie Island

WHERE TO SEE: Widespread and common in most plant communities, especially in mires, bogs, late snow beds, and pool margins (sometimes forming a floating mat extending 1–2 m from the shore); also in drier fellfield habitats and on dry moss turf dominated by *Polytrichum strictum*.

ALTITUDE: 0–200 m.

2 Lesser Rush
Juncus inconspicuus

Very similar, but much smaller in all characters, to the Greater Rush, from which it is difficult to distinguish. The cylindrical pointed leaves are short (0·5–2·0 cm), dark to reddish green and with inconspicuous flowers (1–2) borne amongst the leaves. The anthers are the most prominent part of the flower. The small seed capsule is oval. Due to its diminutive stature and similarity to short forms of the Greater Rush, it is easily overlooked.

Native

GR: Patagonia, Falkland Islands

WHERE TO SEE: It is much less common than Greater Rush, occurring in dry gravelly habitats, notably glacial outwash areas, river terraces, moraines and late snow beds.

ALTITUDE: 15–150 m.

3 Brown or Magellanic Rush
Rostkovia magellanica

The dark brownish green, 8–15 (25) cm long, erect, rigid, sharply pointed leaves arise from a trailing underground rhizome. The leaf is a flattened cylinder in section. The solitary terminal flowers (5–8 mm) are borne on a 5–15 cm tall stem and have a pale margin and prominent anthers (*left inset*). In late summer these produce a conspicuous reddish-brown to black, shiny, globular seed capsule (*right inset*).

Native

GR: Patagonia, Falkland Islands

WHERE TO SEE: Widespread and abundant, especially on the mid-north coast, where it commonly forms extensive mire and bog communities on wet level areas, valley floors, seepage slopes, and lake, pool and stream margins; less frequently on dry stony ground amongst Brown Fescue.

ALTITUDE: 0–225 (300) m.

In addition to the well-established alien plants, numerous other species have been introduced to South Georgia. Some have persisted for many years within or close to whaling stations. However, they are either of very sporadic occurrence or are growing in locations unlikely to be visited. Several species that occurred at Grytviken for many years between the mid-1960s and early 1970s have subsequently disappeared. Some have recently reappeared, from buried seeds, as a result of the ground being disturbed during the recent clean-up and other work at the station.

FORBS (non-grasslike herbs)

Shepherd's Purse
Capsella bursa-pastoris
A few plants at King Edward Point. Annual. Unlikely to persist.

Square-stemmed St.John's-wort
Hypericum tetrapterum
Single plant. Husvik. Probably deliberately introduced.

Chickweed *Stellaria media*
Reappeared at Grytviken around 2004. Annual. Unlikely to persist.

Procumbent Pearlwort
Sagina procumbens
Numerous plants. Grytviken, Husvik, Leith. Reappeared at Grytviken in 2002 and spreading rapidly.

White Clover *Trifolium repens*
Several small colonies. Grytviken, Husvik, Leith.

Lady's Mantle *Alchemilla monticola*
Single plant. Husvik.

Cow Parsley *Anthriscus sylvestris*
Two plants known, Grytviken, Husvik. One at Grytviken produced numerous offspring in the 1990s but by 2010 appeared to be declining in vigour.

Curled Dock *Rumex crispus*
Three individuals at Grytviken – one in front of church was destroyed in 2009, one at Husvik.

Diddledee *Empetrum rubrum*
Single large plant near Grytviken. Origin Falkland Islands. Possibly deliberately introduced.

Thyme-leaved Speedwell
Veronica serpyllifolia
Reappeared at two sites at Grytviken about 2002.

Creeping Pratia *Pratia repens*
Two populations. Grytviken, near Husvik. Origin Falkland Islands. Probably deliberately introduced.

Sneezewort *Achillea ptarmica*
Husvik, Stromness and Leith Harbour whaling stations.

Hawkweed *Leontodon autumnalis*
Single plant, Husvik. Probably deliberately introduced.

White Clover

Creeping Pratia

Mat Grass

Thyme-leaved Speedwell

Procumbent Pearlwort

Marsh Sedge

GRASSES

Couch Grass *Elymus repens*
Several patches. Grytviken, Husvik, Leith.

Sheep's Fescue *Festuca ovina*
Several small patches. Husvik, Ocean Harbour.

Wavy Hair-grass *Deschampsia flexuosa*
Several small patches. Husvik.

Spiked Trisetum *Trisetum spicatum*
A large population near Stromness.

Brown Bent-grass *Agrostis vinealis*
Two or more populations. Grytviken.

Sweet Vernal Grass
Anthoxanthum odoratum
Single population of several patches. Near Husvik.

Mat Grass *Nardus stricta*
Single plants. Leith, near Maiviken.

SEDGES

Marsh Sedge *Carex aquatilis*
Single large population. Husvik.

Common Sedge *Carex nigra*
Several populations. Husvik, Ocean Harbour.

Sedge *Carex* sp.
Single plant, Husvik. Probably deliberately introduced.

173

① Brittle Bladder-fern
Cystopteris fragilis

The yellowish green, feathery tapering fronds (10–20 cm long) of this fern arise in clusters from a dark brown scaly rhizome. Each frond has a brittle black stem with a row of finely divided leaflets on either side, decreasing towards the tip. Clusters of fine brown spores are borne on the underside of some fronds.

Native

GR: Worldwide

WHERE TO SEE: Widespread but not common, mainly in inland rock crevices and at the junction between screes and cliffs.

ALTITUDE: 5–225 (375) m.

② Adder's-tongue
Ophioglossum crotalophoroides

Each plant comprises a single, fleshy, yellow-green, concave frond, up to 4 cm long by 2 cm wide, that tapers to a blunt point (*bottom image*). Fronds are borne on a fleshy stem up to 5 cm long but often hidden in moss. Individual plants arise from a swollen fleshy underground rhizome. Spores are produced in a yellow-green cylindrical, ribbed structure (sporangium), 5–15 mm long, borne on a 2–6 cm erect stalk arising from the centre of the elliptical frond (*top image*).

Native

GR: Patagonia, Falkland Islands, Tristan da Cunha, Central and North America

WHERE TO SEE: An elusive, inconspicuous and rather rare species usually found in short *Juncus* and moss-dominated flushes and seepage areas.

ALTITUDE: 15–150 m.

③ Falklands Filmy Fern
Hymenophyllum falklandicum

A tiny (0·5–3·0 cm tall), delicate plant with a wiry, intertwining black rhizome. The fronds resemble a leafy liverwort, but are dark green and translucent. They are borne on very short stems and the individual leaflets may be bilobed with distinctly serrated margins. Spores are produced in a 1 mm diameter, dark brown or black, globular capsule.

Native

GR: Patagonia, Falkland Islands, Juan Fernandez Islands

WHERE TO SEE: Widespread, seldom very frequent, inconspicuous, growing in damp shaded rock crevices and rock overhangs.

ALTITUDE: 3–350 (500) m.

④ Strap Fern
Grammitis poeppigiana

This diminutive fern has short, dark green, strap-like, smooth-edged fronds, up to 3 cm long by 0·5 cm wide. Fronds are narrowest at the base and end in a slightly rounded tip. Tiny linear clusters of brown spores occur on either side of the central vein on the underside of the upper half of the leaves.

Native

GR: Patagonia, Falkland Islands, southern Africa, southern Australia, New Zealand and offshore islands, subantarctic islands

WHERE TO SEE: A rare plant, easily overlooked, growing in shaded rock crevices and beneath rock overhangs in inland cliffs.

ALTITUDE: 10–375 m.

174

Shield Fern
Polystichum mohrioides

Plants consist of clumps of erect, rigid, bright green leathery fronds up to 25 cm long, usually surrounded by a mass of dead brown foliage of previous years. Fronds have a large number of overlapping leaflets (pinnae) arranged along both sides of the main stem, the lower ones being serrated. The leaf stems are clothed with dark brown scales. The unfurling young fronds are distinctly crozier-shaped. Circular clusters of brown spores occur on the underside of the leaflets.

Native

GR: Patagonia, Falkland Islands

WHERE TO SEE: Widespread, locally frequent, but seldom abundant. Typical of inland dry screes and rock ledges, at the junction between cliffs and screes, and at the base of large boulders on hillsides.

ALTITUDE: 10–375 m.

Small Fern
Blechnum penna-marina

A small compact fern with two types of frond. The almost prostrate basal, sterile pinnate fronds, 5–15 cm long, form a rosette arising from underground rhizomes. Each frond has many leaflets (pinnae) along the leaf stem. Similar but much longer erect spore-bearing fronds rise from the basal mat, unfurling in a crozier shape in spring. Both types of frond are dark shiny green, but in spring are strongly tinged with red. On either side of the central vein on the underside of each pinna on the fertile fronds is a row of brown spore clusters.

Native

GR: Patagonia, Falkland Islands, subantarctic islands

WHERE TO SEE: Very local, mainly among open *Festuca* and *Acaena* communities, occasionally in fine scree and river-bed shingle. Known only from the north side of Busen Peninsula and Husdal, near Husvik.

ALTITUDE: 10–75 m.

Magellanic Clubmoss
Lycopodium magellanicum

A much-branched creeping plant with yellowish to pale green triangular, rigid, scale-like leaves along the trailing stems (10–50 cm long). Cylindrical, erect, pale green, scaly, spore-producing 'cones' (strobili), 1·5–3·0 cm long, are borne on the ends of some short branches. After spore dispersal the withered cones become pale brown. In late summer the plants develop an autumnal tinge of bright reddish-orange. This is the only South Georgia plant to undergo such a seasonal change in colour.

Native

GR: Patagonia, Juan Fernandez Islands, Falkland Islands, subantarctic islands

WHERE TO SEE: Widespread and locally frequent, especially in dry stony fellfield communities on glacial and river outwash areas with developing vegetation.

ALTITUDE: 5–250 m.

This category of plants includes mosses and liverworts (collectively referred to as bryophytes), fungi, algae and lichens. They reproduce by spores that develop in specialised structures, not by seeds developing in flowers. They lack the specialised tissues possessed by higher plants. Virtually none of these plants has a common name.

Andreaea sp.

Mosses

About 120 species of mosses have been identified on South Georgia, of which less than 5% are considered endemic. Most are difficult to identify without specialist knowledge or microscopic examination, but several are common and are important constituents of some of the principal plant communities. All bryophytes grow as a mass of shoots, most forming a dense erect turf (in dry to moist habitats), small compact cushions (on dry rock surfaces) or prostrate intertwining mats (in wet habitats). Only a few of the most prominent species are given here.

Andreaea species

WHERE TO SEE: Frequently grow on stones and boulders in fellfield communities and on dry rock faces All avoid habitats influenced by seabirds and seals and are more typical of inland and higher altitude sites.

ALTITUDE: 5–1,000 m.

Several species of this dark brown to blackish (when dry), compact cushion-forming moss (approx. 2–8 cm diameter). However, without close inspection these can be confused easily with other small, dark cushion-forming genera, e.g. *Grimma*, *Schistidium* and *Racomitrium*, all of which may occur together.

Brachythecium austrosalebrosum

WHERE TO SEE: Locally common in wet habitats.

ALTITUDE: 3–200 m.

This prominent moss forms a very loose turf or tall hummock of golden-yellow shoots in mires, along streamsides and on wet rocks and ledges, usually among other wet habitat mosses. The fleshy, wick-like stems are up to 20 cm long.

Chorisodontium aciphyllum

WHERE TO SEE: Frequently found amongst Tussock Grass on moist slopes near the shore, but more scattered in both dry fescue grassland and bog communities.

ALTITUDE: 2–200 m.

A common turf-forming moss with loosely packed, erect, pointed green shoots with the terminal leaves tapering to a fine point resembling a watercolour paintbrush. Its long, narrow pointed leaves curve to one side of the stem. The soft turf banks can reach 50+ cm in height and overlie a loose fibrous peat.

The closely-related *Dicranoloma*

Chorisodontium aciphyllum

subimponens forms a dark golden green short turf understorey in wet Brown Rush communities.

Pohlia wahlenbergii

WHERE TO SEE: Locally common.

ALTITUDE: 2–150 m.

This distinctive reddish-stemmed moss forms a loose turf of very pale yellowish green shoots, 3–8 cm tall, mainly along the margins of streams and around springs. It is almost indistinguishable from *Philonotis acicularis* growing in the same habitat and often intermixed with *Pohlia* but differs in its blackish stems.

Pohlia wahlenbergii surrounded by *Brachythecium austrosalebrosum*

Conostomum pentastichum

WHERE TO SEE: Frequent in various stages of dry to moist Brown Fescue grassland, fellfield and rock ledges.

ALTITUDE: 2–250 m.

A bright to yellow-green moss that typically forms discrete hard cushions up to 7–8 cm high and 10–30 cm diameter but often coalescing to form a compact mat of circular colonies. It may be recognised by the leaves being arranged in five rows along the stem. This gives the apex, when viewed from above, a star-shaped appearance.

Conostomum pentastichum

Polytrichum strictum

WHERE TO SEE: It forms locally extensive hummocky turves amongst dry tussac grassland and adjacent to dry fescue grassland.

ALTITUDE: 5–150 m.

The robust densely-packed erect shoots form a hard turf, up to 50 cm or more deep, overlying a fibrous peat. The bright green, rigid, waxy leaves (3–6 mm long) at each shoot tip have a star-like appearance.

Several closely related species are also common on dry gravelly soil but they only form small, short loose (2–10 cm

Polytrichum strictum

tall) turves, often in circular patches, and the individual shoots resemble miniature fir trees (e.g. *Polytrichum juniperinum*, *P. piliferum*, *Polytrichastrum alpinum*).

Racomitrium lanuginosum

WHERE TO SEE: Frequent on inland, dry, windswept boulders, rock outcrops and stony fellfield communities.

ALTITUDE: 10–500 m.

This distinctive moss forms loose cushion-shaped (up to 30 cm diameter) aggregations of silvery-grey shoots. Individual leaves have a long whitish 'hair point' extending from the tip.

Racomitrium lanuginosum

Sanionia uncinata

WHERE TO SEE: Most typical of wet habitats, notably in bog, mire and lakeside communities, but also scattered in drier communities, fellfield, rock ledges etc.

ALTITUDE: 1–250 m.

A common, compact to straggling, mat-forming yellow green moss, the leaves being distinctly hook-shaped and all curving in the same direction along the stem. Almost inseparable from *S. austro-georgica* with which it also occurs.

Sanionia uncinata

Syntrichia robusta

WHERE TO SEE: It often occurs as a continuous understorey in mire and open Greater Burnet communities.

ALTITUDE: 2–250 m.

A very common and widespread moss with soft, slightly reflexed leaves, recognised by its rusty-brown colour. Its terminal leaves have a star–shaped appearance. The shoots form a loose turf up to 6–8 cm tall.

Syntrichia robusta

Warnstorfia sarmentosa

WHERE TO SEE: Most abundant in bogs and less so in mires.

ALTITUDE: 2–150 m.

Similar to *Sanionia* but it is dark golden to blackish-green and has straight, elongated leaves, the terminal ones giving each stem a pointed appearance. A related species, *Warnstorfia laculosum*, usually with dark green and much denser shoots and smaller leaves, occurs in the wettest bogs, often with *W. sarmentosum* and also *S. uncinata*.

Warnstorfia sarmentosa

Liverworts

Most of about 100 species of liverwort are inconspicuous and usually grow among mosses, with less than 5% being endemic. Most are moss-like, with tiny leaves arranged on each side of a stem. Unlike mosses, their leaves are often divided into two or more rounded or pointed lobes and have no central vein. These usually bear small 1–2 mm fringed cups which produce gemmae for vegetative reproduction

The most prominent species is the **Strap Liverwort** *Marchantia berteroana*.

WHERE TO SEE: It usually forms compact hard mats on damp banks of streams and where late snowbanks lie, as well as around the base of tussac pedestals in elephant seal wallow areas.

ALTITUDE: 2–125 m.

This plant comprises a leathery, bright green branching thallus (1–4 cm by 1·0–1·5 cm), often tinged purple at the margins and bearing small 'cups'.

Marchantia berteroana

Freshwater alga

Algae

This group of plants includes many forms ranging from unicellular species to the multicellular seaweeds, including the massive kelp (*Macrocystis pyrifera*) which reaches over 30 m in length. Although there are very many unicellular species in the soil and fresh water, and many straggling larger forms in streams and pools, the only conspicuous terrestrial macroalga is *Prasiola crispa*. This comprises masses of small, 0·5–2·5 cm, dark green leaf-like structures, invariably associated with muddy areas disturbed and enriched by seals and seabirds near the shore. These aggregations form dense patches, sometimes covering hundreds of square metres, mostly from 1–50 m altitude.

Aggregations of single-celled snow algae tinge melting snowbanks and glaciers pink or green in late summer.

Prasiola crispa on abandoned Gentoo colony.

Lichens

Lichens are not strictly plants but a symbiotic combination of an alga and a fungus. The fungus forms the body of the lichen which is called a thallus. Most lichens avoid wet habitats and many survive in extreme conditions of drought and high or low temperature, and rapid fluctuations in all of these. They obtain most of their water by absorption from the atmosphere. There are three main growth forms: crustose (encrusting rock or soil), fruticose (multibranched bushy forms) and foliose (narrow, overlapping, lobed branchlets to larger leaf-like structures). About 200 species are known on South Georgia but, like the mosses and liverworts, most lichens are very difficult to identify without microscopic examination. Almost 25% of the lichen species are endemic to the island. In areas grazed by Reindeer, most of the larger (macrolichen) species have been virtually eradicated. Only the most prominent lichens are noted here.

Caloplaca and *Xanthoria* species

ALTITUDE: 0–100 m, occasionally higher.

Coastal rocks and cliffs are commonly, and often extensively, coloured bright orange by several crustose species of *Caloplaca* and *Xanthoria*. These lichens favour the high nitrogen (ammonia) input from nearby colonies of penguins and other seabirds. They are also tolerant of high concentrations of salt from sea spray. Numerous less conspicuous crustose species are also associated with bird colonies. Such species also colonise boulders used as perches by birds (e.g. by skuas, gulls and terns), often quite far inland.

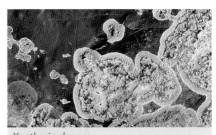

Xanthoria elegans

Boulder used as a perch by birds covered with nitrogen-loving lichens.

Cladonia cf. carneola 'pyxie cups'

Cladonia bellidiflora

Cladonia cf. borealis

Cladonia rangiferina

Pyxie cup lichens *Cladonia* species

WHERE TO SEE: Most grow among dry fescue grassland, but many species are widely distributed in most other communities, except the wettest.

ALTITUDE: The majority occur at lower altitudes but some extend to over 350 m.

This is one of the largest genera on the island with 23 species, many being difficult to differentiate. Many species have a small foliose base from which arises a stalk called a podetium, with a trumpet-shaped 'cup' at the tip, although some species lack this and end in a point. Podetia vary in shape, size (up to 10 cm tall) and colour (mostly grey, brown, pale green and pale yellow).

Reindeer Lichen *Cladonia rangiferina*

WHERE TO SEE: Commonest among dry fescue grassland but also frequent on moss turf banks. (*C. pycnoclada*, a similar but finer-branched, pale yellow species, occurs in very short fescue grassland and fellfield but is relatively rare.)

ALTITUDE: 5–350 m.

One of the most distinctive *Cladonia* species, this fruticose species is also common in the Arctic where it is a favourite food of Reindeer, as it is on South Georgia, and Caribou. It forms circular patches, up to about 30 cm diameter, often coalescing and comprising a loose mass of entangled, grey-brown antler-like branchlets.

Pseudocyphellaria freycinetii

WHERE TO SEE: Commonest in dry fescue grassland, open fellfield and rock ledges, as well as on *Polytrichum* and *Chorisodontium* turf banks. (The closely related and very similar, but blue-grey *P. endochrysa* also occurs in fescue grassland and among *Chorisodontium* turf.)

ALTITUDE: 5–300 m.

This is possibly the most spectacular and unmistakable lichen. It has a large multilobed, pale yellow, crinkly foliose thallus. Individuals may be up to 25–30 cm across.

Pseudocyphellaria freycinetii

Map Lichen *Rhizocarpon geographicum*

WHERE TO SEE: Common on stones, scree and any rock surfaces.

ALTITUDE: 10–1,000 m.

A greenish yellow, rock-encrusting thallus, edged and interspersed with black lines, this lichen is typical of dry inland rocks uninfluenced by seabirds. It occurs with various brown, grey and white crustose lichens, often creating an attractive mosaic on rock surfaces.

Coral Lichen *Sphaerophorus globosus*

WHERE TO SEE: Frequent on *Polytrichum* and *Chorisodontium* turf banks and rock ledges.

ALTITUDE: 5–150 m.

A distinctive species resembling *Cladonia rangiferina* but with a more brittle, rusty-pink, coral-like, multi-branched fruticose growth form. Individual colonies are often dome-shaped and may reach 20–25 cm diameter and 7 cm high.

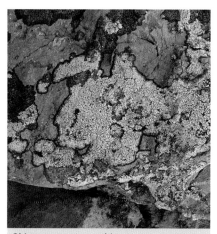

Rhizocarpon geographicum

Sphaerophorus globosus

Stereocaulon alpinum

Stereocaulon glabrum

Usnea antarctica

Usnea aurantiaco-atra

Stereocaulon alpinum

WHERE TO SEE: Frequent in dry Fescue grassland, fellfield, rock ledges, and less so on *Polytrichum* and *Chorisodontium* turf banks.

ALTITUDE: 5–500 m.

This white species forms brittle clumps of erect branches subdivided into very short branchlets, the whole giving the appearance of a cauliflower head. Individuals may reach 10–30 cm diameter and up to 7 cm tall. *S. glabrum* is very similar and occupies the same habitats but is greyish.

Beard lichens *Usnea* species

These fruticose lichens are attached to rock surfaces by a 'holdfast' at the base of the main stem, from which the finely-branched, bushy thallus is borne. These may reach 5 (exceptionally 10) cm in height. *U. antarctica* is typically greyish and is commonest at lower altitudes (2–150 m) while the more robust yellow-grey *U. aurantiaco-atra* tends to occur at higher altitudes (50–700 m). The latter species usually has black, spore-producing discs, 5–10 mm in diameter, at the end of some branches.

Turgidosculum complicatulum

WHERE TO SEE: Abundant on most coastal rocks, forming patches of several square metres, often within the spray zone. It is usually associated with several species of crustose lichens and *Prasiola crispa*.

ALTITUDE: 1–50 m, occasionally over100 m on exposed sea cliffs.

This short (1–2 cm tall), blackish (crisp when dry but gelatinous when wet) cluster of leafy lobes is attached to coastal rocks. It is the lichenised form of the

Turgidosculum complicatulum surrounded by orange Caloplaca.

Agaricus campestris

terrestrial alga *Prasiola crispa* (*page 182*). It is one of very few macroalgae worldwide that forms an association with a fungus to form a lichen, and one of very few non-crustose lichens to inhabit wet habitats.

Fungi

There are several dozen macrofungi (mushrooms and toadstools) on South Georgia but all are small and usually go unnoticed. Most are difficult to identify in the field. They generally grow in damp or boggy areas among moss at low altitude, usually appearing in late summer. Several species of pale to dark brown toadstools, 2–4 cm tall with 1–3 cm diameter caps, are sometimes prolific in bog and mire communities (e.g. *Galerina* spp., *Hypholoma* spp., *Omphalina* spp.). Probably the largest species are the inkcap toadstools (*Coprinus martini*, *C. stercoreus*), 3–6 cm tall, which have a prominent white sausage-shaped cap with a frilly margin. The cap soon decays into an inky black mass. In recent years several Edible Mushrooms (*Agaricus campestris*) have been found, possibly introductions.

Omphalina antarctica

Coprinus martini

187

Taxonomic notes

Confusion can be caused by different names being used for a single species. If you are used to one name for a bird, it can be difficult to find it in a book that is using another name. For instance, sheathbills seen on the shores of South Georgia have been variously called the Snowy, Greater, Pink-faced, American, Wattled and Yellow-billed Sheathbill. The second species of sheathbill is the Lesser or Black-faced.

The confusion caused by a variety of common names is usually prevented by the use of Latin-based scientific names. The sheathbill at South Georgia is *Chionis albus* and its Indian Ocean relative *Chionis minor*. However, scientific names may be changed when new evidence emerges about the relationships between species. Until 1996, the Black-browed Albatross was *Diomedea melanophrys*, closely related to the Wandering Albatross *D. exulans*. Then studies showed that they are not so closely related and the Black-browed Albatross, together with other smaller albatrosses or mollymauks, is now placed in the genus *Thalassarche*.

Genetic techniques are having a great impact on nomenclature through reappraisal of relationships within and between species, and especially the higher level classification of birds and other groups. To avoid confusion, we are mainly following the 'traditional' classification still used in many recent publications.

BIRDS

For species whose breeding range is primarily South American, we follow the recommendations of the South American Classification Committee (SACC) (http://www.museum.lsu.edu/~remsen/SACCBaseline.html). For other species, we follow the recommendations of BirdLife International (http://www.birdlife.org/datazone/species).

New studies of the relationships between the major groups of birds have resulted in a rearrangement in the sequence of orders, but we are using the conventional sequence to avoid confusion and make it easier to compare with other guide books.

Rockhopper Penguin It is now widely accepted there are two species: Northern *(Eudyptes moseleyi)* and Southern *(E. chrysocome)*, with the latter at South Georgia (and the Falklands).

Royal Penguin Despite clear differences in face colour and small differences in measurements, this is sometimes treated as a subspecies of Macaroni Penguin. This is because of the occurrence of dark-faced (Macaroni-like) individuals at Macquarie Island (which could be evidence of interbreeding) and relatively small genetic differentiation.

For albatrosses generally, we follow the recommendations of the Taxonomic Working Group of the Agreement on the Conservation of Albatrosses & Petrels (ACAP) (**http://www.acap.aq/english/english/working-groups/taxonomy-working-group**), particularly in recognising several species in each of the Wandering Albatross and White-capped Albatross complexes.

Wandering Albatross Most of the old subspecies of Wandering Albatross *Diomedea exulans* are now regarded as separate species; at South Georgia only *D. exulans* occurs, which was sometimes also referred to as the Snowy Albatross *D. e. chionoptera*.

White-capped Albatross *Thalassarche steadi* is distinct from Shy Albatross *T. cauta*.

Kerguelen Petrel Now known as *Aphrodroma brevirostris* rather than *Lugensa*.

Great-winged Petrel Some authorities treat this as distinct from Grey-faced Petrel *Pterodroma (macroptera) gouldi* of New Zealand.

Snow Petrel Some authorities separate the Greater *Pagodroma confusa* from the Lesser *P. nivea* Snow Petrel, through differences in size (no overlap in main measurements) and behaviour. Only Lesser Snow Petrel *P. nivea* is reported from South Georgia.

Great and Sooty Shearwaters Genetic data suggest that these shearwaters should be placed in the genus *Ardenna* rather than *Puffinus,* but authorities currently differ in accepting this.

Little Shearwater Birds seen in the South Atlantic are almost certainly Subantarctic Little Shearwaters *Puffinus (assimilis) elegans*, which breed at Tristan da Cunha and Gough and on New Zealand subantarctic islands and is accorded species status in some recent treatments.

Common Diving-petrel South Georgia birds belong to the subantarctic subspecies *Pelecanoides urinatrix exsul*. Different subspecies breed in the Falklands and at Tristan da Cunha and Gough.

Great Egret Old World and New World forms may be separate species; New World birds would then be known as Western Great Egret *Ardea alba.*

Cattle Egret The form that colonised the New World over 100 years ago came from populations now known as the Western Cattle Egret *Bubulcus ibis*, often now regarded as a species distinct from Asian populations.

Imperial Shag The taxonomy of shags is controversial. The King Shag *Phalacrocorax albiventer* and Blue-eyed Shag *P. atriceps*, or collectively the Imperial Shag *P. atriceps*, form a complex across southern South America, Scotia Arc, Antarctic Peninsula and subantarctic islands. Distinctions mainly rest on size, the demarcation between the black and white facial plumage and the extent of white on shoulders and back. Given the lack of modern studies of the shags' morphology, plumage and genetics, we consider the South Georgia Shag to be a subspecies *georgianus* (South Georgia, South Sandwich Islands and South Orkney Islands) of the Imperial Shag. These shags are sometimes placed in the genus *Leucocarbo* with a group of somewhat similar shags of southern New Zealand and its subantarctic islands.

South Georgia Pintail Often treated as a subspecies of Yellow-billed Pintail *Anas g. georgica* but we treat it as a full species, based on differences in plumage, measurements and number of tail feathers.

Peregrine Birds seen at South Georgia belong to the distinctive race *Falco p. cassini* of southern South America and the Falkland Islands.

Brown Skua Recent genetic research has shown that the two genera of skuas – *Catharacta* and *Stercorarius* – should be combined into *Stercorarius*. The taxonomy of the 'Southern Skua' *S. antarcticus* complex is still rather controversial, largely due to interbreeding where different skuas mix. Most specialists agree that South Polar Skua *S. maccormicki*, Chilean Skua *S. chilensis* and Brown Skua *S. antarcticus* are species (and distinct from Great Skua *S. skua* of the northern hemisphere). However, there are distinct populations of Brown Skua in the Falkland Islands and south-east Argentina (*S. a. antarcticus*), Tristan da Cunha and Gough (*S. a. hamiltoni*) and at South Georgia south to the Antarctic Peninsula and east to the subantarctic islands of the Indian Ocean and New Zealand (*S. a. lonnbergi*).

Gulls The old genus *Larus* has been split so Kelp Gull remains as *Larus*, while Dolphin and Franklin's Gulls are now *Leucophaeus* and Brown-headed Gull is *Chroicocephalus.*

Antarctic Tern The subspecies at South Georgia *Sterna vittata georgiae* is distinctly smaller (but longer-winged) and darker than other subspecies.

Barn Owl Recent genetic studies suggest that American forms of the Barn Owl may be distinct species from Old World forms. If so, the subspecies of eastern South America and the Falkland Islands (*Tyto a. tuidara*) would become a subspecies of American Barn Owl *T. furcata*.

Barn Swallow All individuals seen at South Georgia are believed to belong to the New World subspecies *Hirundo rustica erythrogaster*.

Chilean Swallow Recent studies show that the correct species name is *Tachycineta leucopyga*, not *T. meyeni* or *Hirundo leucopyga*, which was widely used since the 1970s.

MARINE MAMMALS

The most up-to-date classification of marine mammals is the 'List of marine mammal species and subspecies. Society for Marine Mammalogy's Committee on Taxonomy. 2009.' This can be seen on their website www.marinemammalscience.org.

For common and scientific names we are using the very similar 'Marine mammals of the world: Systematics and distribution.' Rice, D. 1998. Special Publication Number 4. The Society for Marine Mammalogy, Lawrence, KS. 231p. 1998.

INVERTEBRATES

Land Snail *Notodiscus hookeri* Identification provisional pending further research.

PLANTS

No up-to-date published classification of plants covers South Georgia plants, but the following older publications may suffice, although some specific names have since changed.

Greene, S.W. & Walton D.W.H. 1975. An annotated check list of the sub-antarctic and antarctic vascular flora. *Polar Record*, 17, 473–484.

Øvstedal, D.O. & Lewis-Smith, R.I. 2001. *Lichens of Antarctica and South Georgia. A Guide to their Identification and Ecology.* Cambridge University Press, Cambridge, 411 pp + 104 plates and 50 figures.

Ochyra, R., Lewis-Smith, R.I. & Bednarek-Ochyra, H. 2008. *The Illustrated Moss Flora of Antarctica.* Cambridge University Press, Cambridge, 685 pp + 42 plates & 275 figures.

RECENT NAME CHANGES

NATIVES

Tussock Grass *Poa flabellata* formerly known as *Parodiochloa flabellata*

Magellanic Foxtail *Alopecurus magellanicus* formerly *A. antarcticus*

Smith's Sedge *Uncinia macrolepis* formerly *U. meridensis* and before *ca.* 1980 *U. smithii*

Strap Fern *Grammitis poeppigiana* formerly *G. kerguelensis*

ALIENS

Mouse-ear Chickweed *Cerastium fontanum* formerly *C. holosteoides*

Common Bent-grass *Agrostis capillaris* sometimes *A. tenuis*

Tufted Hair-grass *Deschampsia cespitosa* formerly *D. caespitosa*

Couch Grass *Elymus repens* formerly *Agropyron repens*

Bittercress *Cardamine* sp. Identity uncertain. First considered as Hairy Bittercress *Cardamine hirsuta* but now thought to be *C. glacialis* of Patagonia and Falkland Islands.

Glossary

Auricular	Area around the ear opening of a bird.
Awn	Bristle on a seed or grass flower.
Axil	Angle between the upper surface of a branch or leaf stalk and the stem from which it grows.
Bryophyte	Group of plants that includes mosses and liverworts.
Cere	Waxy, often brightly coloured, fleshy area at the base of a bird's bill.
Endemic	Confined to a certain region.
Forb	Herbaceous plant that is not a grass, sedge or rush.
Gadfly petrel	Medium to large petrel of the genus *Pterodroma*.
Gorget	A crescent-shaped, coloured patch on the neck of a bird.
Graminoid	Any, usually herbaceous, plant with narrow leaves growing from the base, including grasses, sedges and rushes.
Herb	Any flowering plant without a woody stem. Includes forbs and graminoids.
Inflorescence	The flower-bearing part of a plant.
Mandible	The upper or lower half of a bird's bill.
Mollymawk	One of a group of medium-sized albatrosses of the genus *Thalassarche*.
Nototheniid	One of a large group of fishes found only in the Southern Ocean.
Nectary	A glandular structure secreting nectar at the base of some flower petals.
Podetia	Stalks bearing the fruit in some lichens.
Polychaete	A group of mainly seawater worms with paired appendages on each segment.
Undertail coverts	Short feathers under the base of a bird's tail, often useful for identification.

Acknowledgements

Text was provided by

Robert Burton	Topography and Geology, Climate, The Fertile Sea, South Sandwich Islands
Darren Christie	History of Exploitation, Introduced animals & plants, Biosecurity, Habitat Restoration, Protected Areas and Regulations, Introduced Mammals
John Croxall	Preface, Taxonomic Notes (birds)
Ari Friedlaender	Cetaceans
Roger Key	Invertebrates
Ron Lewis-Smith	Vegetation and Communities, Plants, Taxonomic Notes (plants)
Tony Martin	Seals, Ducks
Richard Phillips	Tubenoses, Skuas
Norman Ratcliffe	Other birds
Phil Trathan	Penguins

The British Antarctic Survey provided the maps.

Robert Burton thanks the following for generous assistance with advice and specialist information: Jonathan Ashburner, Andy Black, Darren Christie, Andrew Clarke, Peter Convey, Márcia Engel, Dick Filby, Bob Flood, Larry Hobbs, Morten Jørgensen, Denise Landau, Pat and Sarah Lurcock, Tony Marr, Stephanie Martin, Tony Martin, Richard McKee, Michael Moore, Alison Neil, Robert Pitman, Sally Poncet, Jonathan Shanklin, John Splettstoesser, Phil Trathan, and in particular John Croxall and Ron Lewis-Smith.

At **WILD**Guides Robert Still used great skill in laying out the text and illustrations to make the book a practical field guide, Brian Clews checked the proofs for errors and inconsistencies and Andy Swash prepared the index.

Photographic Credits

All photographs used in this book are credited by using the photographer's initials, as follows:

Jon Ashburner/BAS [JA], Andy Black [AB], Sam Bosanquet [SB], British Antarctic Survey [BAS], Robert Burton [RB], Stuart Cable [SCa], Darren Christie [DC], Sam Crimmin/BAS [SCr], Stewart Dodd [SD], Ewan Edwards/BAS [EE], Jaume Forcada/BAS [JF], Dick Filby (**www.rarebirdalert.co.uk**) [DFi], Derren Fox/BAS [DFo], Deirdre Galbraith [DG], Chris Gilbert/BAS [CG], Tony Hall [TH], Richard Harker [RH], Peter Harrison [PH], Alan Henry [AH], Larry Hobbs [LH], Morten Jørgensen [MJ], Luke Kenny/BAS [LK], Roger Key (**key_r_s@yahoo.co.uk**) [RK], Ron Lewis-Smith [RLS], James Lowen [JCL], Pat Lurcock [PL], Sarah Lurcock [SL], Mick Mackey/BAS [MM], Donald Malone [DM], Russ Manning [RM], Tony Martin [TM], Séamus McCann [SM], Paula Olson (courtesy International Whaling Commission) [PO], Joanna Osborne [JO], Paula O'Sullivan/BAS [POS], Phil Palmer (Bird Holidays) [PP], Laura Parrish [LP], Caroline Pearce [CP], A J Pearson [AP], Fabiano Peppes/Albatross Task Force [FP], Ben Phalan/BAS [BP], Robert Pitman [RPi], Rick Price [RPr], Phil Pugh [PPu], Norman Ratcliffe [NR], Mike Richardson [MR], Shallow Marine Surveys Group (**www.smsg-falklands.org**) [SMSG], Jonathan Shanklin/BAS [JS], Elaine Shemilt [ES], Chris Srigley [CS], Brent Stephenson (**www.eco-vista.com**) [BS], Robert Still [RS], David Tipling [DT] (**www.davidtipling.com**), Phil Trathan/BAS [PT], Carol Walton [CW], David Walton/BAS [DW], Allan White [AW], Tony Williams/BAS [TW], David Wilson [DW].

The locations where the images were taken are shown in square brackets and coded as follows: Antarctic[1] [Ant]; Atlantic: North [NAtl], South-west[2] [SWAtl], South [SAtl]; Falkland Islands [Falk]; Gough Island [GoI]; Macquarie Island [MacI]; North America [NAm]; Pacific Sector[3] [Pac]; Scotia Sea [ScS]; Snares Island Sea [SI]; South America [SAm]; Unknown location [-].

[1] Antarctic Peninsula, South Shetlands and Antarctica.
[2] The seas from the Drake Passage eastwards to Tristan da Cunha.
[3] The seas west of the Drake Passage, including Australia, New Zealand and the subantarctic islands.

Cover   King Penguin colony in the snow: DG.

Frontispiece **Wandering Albatross**: DFo.
Page 8   **King Penguins**: EE.
Page 9   **Wandering Albatross**: TM.
Page 10   King Edward Cove: BAS.
Page 11   Glacial Scenery: TM.
Page 12   Lenticular Clouds: CP.
Page 13   **Antarctic Fur Seals** exiting water: MJ.
Page 14   Bellingshausen, South Sandwich Islands: AB.
Page 15   Shag Rocks: RB.
Page 16   Sealer's site: RB.
            Trypot: SGHT.
            Tussac trampled by fur seals: EE.
Page 17   Japanese whalers flensing: RB.
            Whalebones: RB.
Page 18   **Patagonian Toothfish**: JA.
            Black-browed Albatross on baited hook: FP.
Page 19   **Cow Parsley** at Grytviken: JS.
Page 20   Rat eradication areas   SGHT.
            Helicopter with bait-spreader: SCr.
Page 21   Schrader Glacier: TM.

Page 22   Passengers cleaning their boots: CW.
Page 23   Exclosure: DC.
Page 24   Replacement grassland: RLS.
Page 25   Tussac grassland: JS.
Page 26   Dry grassland: RLS.
            Wet grassland: RLS.
Page 27   Bog: RLS.
            Mire: RLS.
Page 28   Herbfield: RLS.
            Fellfield: RLS.
Page 29   Bryophyte flushes, stream and pond margins: RB.
Page 30   Moss turf community: RLS.
            Lichen and moss communities: RLS.
Page 31   **Southern Elephant Seal**: TM.

BIRDS
Page 32   **Macaroni Penguin** colony: DFo [SG].
            White-chinned Petrels: BP [SG].
Page 33   **South Georgia Pintail**: TM [SG].
            Brown Skuas: MJ [SG].
Page 35   **King Penguin**: PT [SG].
Page 36   **King Penguins**: MJ [SG].
Page 37   **King Penguin** (with egg): PL; (moulting): MJ; (chicks): DFo [all SG].

Index of English and scientific names

This index includes the common English and *scientific* names of all the birds, mammals, invertebrates and plants included in this book. The names in **bold** highlight the species that are afforded a full account. Figures in **bold red** refer to the pages on which the main text for the species can be found. Blue numbers indicate other pages on which a photograph or illustration appears. Normal black figures are used to highlight the page(s) on which other key information relating to the species is given.